DEVANGELICAL

"Erika Rae has penned a delightful and compelling meditation on personal reinvention that will both tickle you and make you blush."

—Jonathan Evison, author of *The Revised Fundamentals of Caregiving*, *West of Here*, and *All About Lulu*

"I'm a believer that Erika Rae will make you cackle with heathen delight throughout *Devangelical*. Aside from that, my Mom is going to be so happy I read a book with the word 'Jesus' in it!"

— Laurie Notaro, author of *The Idiot Girl's Action-Adventure Club*, *I Love Everybody (And Other Atrocious Lies)*, and *There's a Slight Chance I Might Be Going to Hell*

"Whether you think Erika Rae is a prophet of truth or a whore of Babylon, you have to admit she's a sinfully sublime writer. Her memoir is a triumph: honest, profound, sexy, and funny as all hell. *Devangelical* is a wicked good book—and I do mean wicked."

— Greg Olear, author of *Fathermucker* and *Totally Killer*

"I swear to God, I couldn't stop reading Erika Rae's *Devangelical*! It is a charming, original, hilarious and insightful trip into the mind and soul of a young Evangelical girl."

— Jessica Anya Blau, author of *Drinking Closer to Home* and *The Summer of Naked Swim Parties*

"A book to make you sad for the entire human race, and yet hopeful for all its individuals."

— Ben Loory, author of *Stories for Nighttime and Some for the Day*

"*Devangelical* is a must read to understand the culture of fundamentalist Christians. Erika Rae shows what goes in inside the minds of teenagers growing up in the faith."

— Tony DuShane, author of *Confessions of a Teenage Jesus Jerk*

"Erika Rae would have gotten me in trouble as a teen. *Devangelical* is the ultimate hysterical note passed down the church pew, eliciting uncontrolled, out-loud laughs in the face of propriety. I fully expected to feel my mother's pinch telling me to shut up and stop giggling."

— Slade Ham, comedian, The Whiskey Brothers comedy group

"This book reads like an exorcism. And I mean that in the best possible way."

— Brad Listi, author of *Attention. Deficit. Disorder.*, founder of The Nervous Breakdown, and host of Other People

DeVaN

A MEMOIR

GELICAL

ERIKA RAE

Emergency Press
New York

Copyright © 2012 by Erika Rae

For information about permissions to reproduce selections from this book, or to order bulk purchases, write to Emergency Press at info@emergencypress.org.

Book design by Kelly Hobkirk
Cover image by Anthony Camera

Rae, Erika
ISBN 978-0-9836932-5-3
1. Nonfiction—Biography & Autobiography. 2. Nonfiction—Personal Memoirs.
3. Nonfiction—Philosophy & Spirituality.

Emergency Press
154 W. 27th St.
#5W
New York NY 10001
emergencypress.org

9 8 7 6 5 4 3 2 1
First printing

Printed in the United States of America
Distributed by Publishers Group West

DEVANGELICAL

A MEMOIR

For Scott, my partner through it all

Author's Note

Memory has a tendency to fold events and personalities into a slow-cooked stew, and mine is no exception. While the people in this memoir are based on real people, most also have flavors and infusions from others. In other words, if you recognize yourself as one of my characters, you are probably at least partly wrong. My former youth leaders suffer the most from this affliction and probably better reflect composites of these dear people than actual representations. "King Richard," for example, is most certainly a combination of at least two different people, both for whom I continue to have great respect. I've done this on purpose in order to protect people and places in some cases, and out of faulty memory in others. Even so, all events in this book are true and recounted as I remember them.

DEVANGELICAL [dee-van-jel-i-kuhl] A person who grew up in—and, consequently, out of—the evangelical thought-stream. May or may not include loss of one's faith, but definitely the loss of one's mind.

Every day people are straying away from the church and going back to God.

— Lenny Bruce

The End of the World

On the last day of the world, I forgot to set my alarm.

"Get up! It's time to go!" came my father's voice, followed by the pounding of footsteps.

I snapped upright in my bed, thinking that it was actually happening—that Jesus had been spotted somewhere over Colorado Springs like the Goodyear Blimp and that there was no time to lose getting into something more respectable than an oversized nightshirt with Snoopy's Woodstock on the front.

When I finally realized that it was the car that was my destination rather than the upper stratosphere, I took a few deep breaths and turned my attention to my closet. Fifteen minutes later, my younger sister and I strapped ourselves into the backseat and we were on the road. In tense silence, Dad navigated the streets through the legions of fish-studded vehicles, all schooling toward their designated places of worship. We might have even made it on time, had we not suddenly been sandwiched into a holding pattern in the right lane between a large church van on the left and a brown Subaru in front of us which bore the bumper sticker, "Do you follow Jesus this closely?".

I glanced up at my parents sitting quietly in the front seat. My father was a tall man with sparkling green eyes and a lung capacity that allowed him the volume to address large groups on the subject of Jesus Christ. He had an easy smile and was prone to bouts of blind optimism, for which I dearly loved him. Like he did every day of the week except for Saturday, he was dressed in suit and tie. His silver hair was in a side part and held in place by five pumps of VO5. My mother sat next to him, her short brown waves swept neatly over her ears. She was dressed smartly in a rust colored dress with nude stockings and black flats. Both Christian academics, they were not nearly as impressed by the imminence of the End of the World as I was. The year was 1988 and they had seen End Times prophecies from within the Evangelical church before. Each time, they explained, people got all riled up over nothing and they were not going to join in the panic.

"It could happen today," Dad admitted, "but really there is no way to know in advance. The Bible says, "No one knows the day or the hour."[1] It could happen *any* day."

I thought about the picture I had seen of Gorbachev's birthmark looking suspiciously like "666." Maybe there was no way to know which exact minute it would happen, but I had read some pretty convincing arguments that we were looking down the barrel of it. I thought back to that birthmark and shuddered.

"Just try not to get your hopes up, dear," my mother added.

We pulled into the church parking lot and my parents marched off to their class where Dad taught Sunday school to a group of adults.

This could be the last time we do this, I thought and headed inside toward my own Sunday school class. As I walked, I was aware of my feet. Would I be taken after this step? How about this

[1]   * Matthew 24:36

one? Would I make it all the way across the church before I was whisked suddenly away into the clouds? Would my boyfriend be there, too? Would my English teacher understand when I was not there to turn in my as-of-yet unwritten essay on Chaucer the next day? I smiled deliciously to myself as I mulled this last one over.

By the time I walked into the service an hour later, I was getting antsy. It was 11 A.M. and still no end of the world. My boyfriend, Scott—the only person with the misfortune to be called by his real name in this memoir—waved at me from a pew and I made my way over to him. I was so overcome by the Holy Spirit that I flushed pink.

> ### ✳ Guide to Churchese
>
> Altar Call – 1. The way a person ends up at the altar. Usually happens at the end of the sermon during prayer and/or music. People go alone, and often end up in prayer clusters. These people may or may not know the person praying, but may be seen listening with intense interest as the prayer purges their soul of all of their sins. 2. A meter by which an evangelist may gage whether he totally rocked—or totally sucked. There is nothing worse for a preacher's ego than an empty altar.

I looked around the church with Scott at my side as if I were seeing it for the first time—the brown carpeted aisles, the beige padded pews, which were comfortable, but not *too* comfortable, the stained glass at the front depicting the life of Jesus at different stages of life on earth. My eyes fell on the kneeling altar that wrapped its way invitingly around the entire front of the church. Scott and I had prayed there a couple of times together. I looked over at him and giggled nervously. I determined I ought to say something to him.

"Want a mint?" I produced a tin from my purse.

"Thank you," he answered, pinching one between his fingers, which brushed mine on the way back out. Scott was tall and intelligent with gorgeous green eyes and blond hair. I swallowed hard and prayed a quick prayer aimed against any lust demons who might be hanging out in the Lord's house. Angels and demons were real, and if Armageddon was kicking off that day, then I could be certain of one thing: there was going to be a final fight for our souls and it wasn't going to be a clean one. One sin—just one wayward thought, even— would make me unclean. And what if it was that exact moment that Jesus came back and I had not had a chance to ask for forgiveness yet? Would I be doomed? Would I miss out on heaven for all eternity?

Just then, the deep, reedy sound of the organ filled the room, causing me to jump like I had been busted for peeking at swimsuit models on the magazines in the checkout line. Pastor Brown burst onto the platform with the enthusiasm of a wrecking ball and everyone stood to sing the first hymn, "When the Roll Is Called Up Yonder."

Next to me, Scott shifted microscopically closer and brushed my arm with his shirtsleeve. A shock of alarm bolted through me and I glanced at him out of the corner of my eye. I needed a trained team of angels and I needed them stat.

"'When the Roll Is Called Up Yonder'—it may not be long, friends, it may not be long," said Pastor Brown somewhat cryptically. Not wanting to seem reactionary, the church leadership was not discussing the Rapture prophecy openly from the pulpit. But we all knew what he was talking about.

More amens.

I didn't have to look around me to be able to sense the mood in the congregation. It was one of excitement. In response to nearly every statement, somebody called out an "Amen!"

or "Hallelujah." I tried channeling my own excitement about sitting next to Scott toward the front of the church. Surely Pastor Brown would say something to send the demons sailing. I knew no demon could withstand the name of Jesus Christ. Surely it was just a matter of time.

"When our beloved Savior walked this earth amongst us two thousand years ago, he made us a promise. He said 'I will return!'"

The congregation shouted various approved phrases of holiness such as "tell it" and "that's right" and someone began clapping. Next to me, Scott fidgeted closer to me so that our shoulders were touching. I suddenly found that I couldn't move.

I reminded myself that I should not be allowing myself to be so distracted in the midst of what was going on—that I was going to need to *focus* if I wasn't going to miss out on the roll call. I stared hard at Pastor Brown, noticing how the perspiration had already begun dripping from his forehead. He pulled out a white handkerchief from his pocket and began mopping his brow.

"The groom is coming to claim his precious bride," he continued, "but the question is, will the bride be ready? Will the bride be pure?"

Scott inched a little closer. My cheeks were radiating heat at this point and I was conscious of beginning to perspire, myself.

He went on to extend the metaphor into how we must not let the groom catch us sleeping and that we must make every effort to prepare for his appearance. This necessarily meant, of course, cleansing ourselves from all that is sinful. In my particular case, it meant scooting a couple of inches to the right.

Finally, he began a sinner's prayer for redemption, which we all prayed in case it hadn't taken the last time we prayed it. If Jesus was coming back, then we had all better make sure that we were on the guest list. I closed my eyes, focusing all of my attention on the spiritual battle I imagined was raging around me.

"Jesus, we hear you calling to us. We know how much you love us and how much you sacrificed for us," said Pastor Brown.

Faces swathed in shimmering light appear at the top of the ceiling. Arrows are poised in the direction of our pew, where I am willing Scott's hand past the hem of my skirt against all that is pure and holy. Instead, he reaches his opposite hand behind his back toward me. I reach my own hand behind my back on the other side and meet his in the middle. My chest convulses with teen delight.

"We accept your gift and thank you for your love. We surrender ourselves to your ultimate purpose."

A tension is rising and a silence rings out through Heaven—for about seven seconds.

"We thank you, oh Lord, for your promise to return for us one day."

Inexplicably, I uncross my legs. Oh, God, I pray—put an end to this torture!!!

"We look forward to that, Dear Lord, and we know that you have conquered death once through your Son. In Your Son Jesus' precious name, Amen."

Screams recede into the bright sunlight. I reach for a Kleenex.

We were then invited to an altar call. Pastor Brown never knew an empty altar. It didn't matter how short the sermon, he could always coax a couple of sinners down and away from the gnashing of teeth. But he has never—and I mean never—had the success he had on that Sunday.

It started with the familiar tune "Just As I Am" coming through the organ in the background of the pastoral prayer. It was a couple of kids from the Youth Group. With people as moved as they were by the thought of Christ's imminent return, it didn't take long for a few more of their friends to join in. I knew I should join them. My own sanctification process had suffered a severe setback that day. But I am ashamed to say that I was not among them. I was still glued to Scott's shoulder.

Longingly, I watched from my paralysis as several more individuals stood from their seats from various places within the sanctuary. Clusters began to form. Friends, families— it didn't matter. All the while Pastor Brown was in the background, begging Christ to come for us sooner rather than later. People were wailing; a few children were crying; I felt like I was dying. What had gone wrong? Had I not prayed for help?

It didn't make sense. I was pretty much the perfect Christian. Well, OK. Not the *perfect* Christian. But I tried really hard. I read my Bible daily. I went to services of one kind or another at least four times a week. I had even quit the Christian school that year so that I could be a better witness for Christ amongst heathen high school kids. Why was I being forsaken in my time of need? Here I was on the last day of the world with all of eternity before me and all I could think about was...*sex*?

Scott chose that instant to reach over and take my hand. Completely in the wide, inappropriate open.

And it was in that moment—that exact moment—that something inside of me began to rebel.

As I sat petrified into a flushing statue of adolescent desire, a thought occurred to me. *I don't want to go yet.*

I was instantly consumed in guilt. What would God think

of me for not being ready? I was supposed to be ready. I had been preparing for this day my entire life.

This world wasn't real. "Real" life was in Heaven. And sometimes this world fought hard to pull me in and make me believe it was real, but I had made sure that I made all of the appropriate substitutions to get me through the cravings. I listened to Christian contemporary music instead of rock n' roll, I went to Christian activities instead of hanging out with the worldly kids, I said "darn" instead of "damn"....

Maybe I could wait it out until the middle, after all. The Tribulation couldn't be that bad, could it? We could dig a secret shelter in my backyard—like a bomb shelter. We would stock it with everything we could possibly need, like food and batteries and toilet paper. And lip balm. Maybe I could open up an underground business—among other Christians who were also in hiding, like we were. I could sell two kinds: plain and cherry. That would be enough.

I wasn't supposed to not want to go yet, but there it was. Like it or not I had thought it in all of its juicy sinfulness. Jesus may have been on his way ready to take us, but I wasn't ready. I wanted to grow up. Go to college. Have sex. Get married. Have sex.... I was supposed to have my whole life ahead of me. And maybe it was with Scott, and maybe it wasn't—I didn't know. The point was, I was only fifteen—and I wanted to find out.

I looked at my watch. It was noon. The last day of the world was only half over.

Praying for Armageddon

IF YOU DIDN'T GROW UP IN THE EVANGELICAL CHURCH LIKE I did, this idea of the end of the world being just around the corner may be a foreign concept. Sure, there are the occasional scares. Y2K was a big one, with people stocking up on canned soup and bottled water to survive the Roman style crash of civilization that was supposed to happen within minutes of Prince's final chorus of "1999." 2011 saw not one but two End of the World predictions from Evangelical radio host, Harold Camping, who channeled thousands of his listeners' dollars into a worldwide billboard campaign guaranteeing a major city near you that "Judgment Day" was coming on May 21st—and when that didn't happen, again on October 21st.

And then there is the Mayan calendar, which predicts the End of the World in December, 2012. Either the poles are supposed to switch, the zombie apocalypse will be unleashed, or the Age of Aquarius is going to begin. Either way, it is supposed to be epic. And if you are reading this after the predicted date, you can see how that went.

But anyone who grew up Evangelical will understand that these 'ends' are different. Sure, they could happen. But it was the Rapture that we were all watching for. It was the Rapture that was going to signal the coming of the real deal.

There is no feeling that can compare to this expectation. It is dark, cool, and as subtle as the wings of a moth. It is standing in a forest of centuries-old pines and being enveloped in a still chill. White leaves cover the damp path and there is a faint rustling overhead. Eyes are everywhere—and nowhere—all at once. Hands wait poised, ready to reach from behind the thin veil that separates our feeble reality from the solidity of that of the eternal... and snatch you without warning.

If you have not yet had the privilege of almost living through the end of the world, I can tell you first-hand that the experience is quite liberating. No more bills, no more homework, no more laundry. No more pain.

Not too long ago I heard a Christian couple in a radio interview say that they wished desperately that the End Times were near, that God would decide enough was enough and pull the plug on planet Earth so that Armageddon, the final war, could be initiated.

They reported that they pray every day for this.

When the interviewer asked why they wanted the world to end, they explained that they have a three-year-old daughter and they don't want her to grow up in this unsafe and sinful world. They would rather she be taken to Heaven so that she would never have to experience any of it.

I understand how they feel. Once a young Evangelical, I remember all too well what it was like to work myself up over the finer points of prophecy. Would the Rapture, *the time when Jesus returned to the earth to take us away with him*, happen in my lifetime? Was it possible to read the warning signs telling when we were about to be whisked away?

The Evangelical brand of Christianity promises the *only* solution to death. Belief in the deity of Jesus Christ and acceptance of the grace offered through his death earns eternal life. Failure to believe earns Hell. The word "Evangelical" originates from the Greek word "ευαγγελιου" (evangelion), which means "good message," or, more commonly, the "good news," which refers to the gospel. As such, the Evangelical church believes in spreading this information about Jesus in order to save other souls from Hell, too. Having been "saved" or "born again," a person still has to endure the physical death of the body, but the essence of "you" is preserved to move on to the next level. In other words, once your body dies, you can never die again. Once you pass that minor hurdle, you are free to leap from tall clouds and run with sharp scissors *all you want*. And if that means a little cinching of the pleasure belt in this life and a few extra choir practices? Well, heavens yes. That's a worthwhile exchange.

Guide to Churchese

Youth Group – 1. A collection of hormonal teenagers meeting at least weekly in order to talk about God, how not to have sex before marriage, and to play wacky games—often involving a blender and a raw fish. 2. A place where hormonal teenagers meet at least weekly to talk about God, play wacky games, and often end up having "sex."

But imagine there is something else. In addition to this all-expense paid trip to paradise, imagine there is possibly another prize behind the door. Not only do you get an eternity of no pain, fear, or suffering for all your nights of staying home from the dance clubs and going home solo on prom night, for a select few—and for a limited time offer only—you won't even have to die. It would be a gate to eternity—short, quick, and completely painless.

As a teenager in the Evangelical church, I was obsessed by the idea that I could be taken at any moment. Already, I was

immortal in my mind, so the idea of eternal life was pretty
obvious. You mean we aren't going to die? (Duh.) Mostly I
wanted to make sure that I got my still cellulite-free butt to
Heaven, thus avoiding spending eternity with red, hairy dudes
with razor sharp horns. (Ew.)

Even so, when I first found out that it was likely going to
happen to me, I may have gotten a little winded.

*

It happened one night at Youth Group. Something was
wrong.

Since our regular Youth Pastor was out, the scepter fell
to Richard to deliver the gospel message, which we fully
expected to be radical and inspiring per usual. A volunteer
at the church, Richard helped out with the Youth Group on
Wednesday nights and taught our Sunday school class each
week. And because that was not enough, he and his wife also
invited us over to their apartment once a week for a Bible
study. They were energetic, genuine to their core, and never
passed up the opportunity to go miles out of their way to live
their faith.

Now, Richard was a handsome man. He was tall and lean
with a narrow face framed by an exceptional blond mullet.
The haircut was not just incidental, mind you—it was the key.
Not just any mullet, it had a life and personality all of its own.
The way the shorter hairs spiked in every direction while the
longer hairs ended in a glorious cascade which clung to his
long neck as he turned his head from side to side, swooshing
out over bare shoulders where the sleeves had been recently
ripped off—that haircut was anything but mediocre. I even
saw one time when a segment had been separated in back over

the other long hairs into a braid, and let me tell you, it was breathtaking. It was rat-tailesque and, yet, was in a class of its own that defied...classification. If Jesus had walked among us in the late 1980s, there is no doubt in my mind that he would have sported just such a mullet. It was all serious and respectfully worshipful in the front, while full of exuberant praise in the back. And like Jesus, Richard didn't care about status or approval—only that we knew *The Truth*. As a result, we were 100% devoted to Richard as if he were our king. What a visionary! What a radical!

Richard played a few rounds of wall ball with us that night, but you could tell that his heart wasn't in it. Afterwards, we all sort of shuffled into the Lion's Den where we would sing some songs.

We started out with gusto singing "Swing Low Sweet Chariot" and "I Am a C-H-R-I-S-T-I-A-N," but by the time we got to "Kumbaya," everyone knew something was off. A couple of the junior high boys started howling and giggling in the back somewhere, and the whole room just fell to pieces. If it weren't for Scott's intervention, the whole night might have been ruined.

"Have some respect, guys," he said to everybody. "What kind of Youth Group is this? Pastor Mark can't even be away for one night?"

That shut everybody up fast. I glanced at my friend, Amy, who bit back a smile. Amy was short like me, and a nonstop tease.

"He's so cute when he's mad," she squeaked in my ear with a sarcastic squeeze of the eyelids, to which I responded by a playful slap on the shoulder. Scott and I had recently gone to the church Valentine's Day potluck together. It had been our first date. I wore a purple corduroy jumper with a lacy, high-necked collar. He wore heart suspenders and a shirt that was about 2 inches too short in the sleeves. The top of my brunette mop was below his shoulders. We looked awesome.

I looked over at Amy, who was watching Scott mischievously with one fingernail in her mouth. She had recently cut her hair into a bob with teased bangs and wore a mini-skirt ensemble from The Gap.

When it was obvious that we had adequately felt the sting of shame, Richard finally roused himself from a near stupor at the back wall and trudged up to the front. He cleared his throat and looked down at his shoes.

"I don't know, guys. I just don't have it in me tonight to stand up here and tell you right from wrong, which you already know, anyway."

It was awful. He looked drained, as if the life had been sapped out of him. His hair, normally standing at attention with the aid of a silver dollar-sized swipe of gel, hung dull and lifeless around his shoulders as if he had not even bothered to tease it. A few people did stand up from their places with the invited prayer requests and praises, but mostly we just sat in pained horror watching him as he shifted from one Converse high top to the other, as if he had no idea how he had gotten there or why. He was frustrated, he said. He had been working so hard on winning the people in his community for Jesus, and wasn't seeing the kind of results he had been hoping for.

When things didn't improve the next week, we kicked the prayer chain into action. When after a full week of premium, Grade-A prayer, things still didn't look up, we became worried. A couple of us even discussed coming up with a serious crisis of faith so that he would have to pay attention, but if that didn't work, then it was hardly worth risking our own souls. We knew Richard wouldn't want that.

And then, a miracle happened. While we were all rushing around trying to give him a reason to snap out of his depression, he found one all by himself. Actually, he found 88.

That year, until that point unbeknownst to us, a man named Edgar Whisenant had released a small booklet entitled *88 Reasons the Rapture Will Be in 1988*. The idea of the Rapture among Christians has caused a variety of reactions throughout history, causing everything from mass hysteria to people quitting their jobs to waiting around on rooftops. There are dozens of famous examples of people incorrectly predicting the date of the Rapture, which would cause a commotion for a while among believers, but then would inevitably fade into the past once nothing happened.

But Whisenant was different. Not only had he presented 88 powerful reasons why the Rapture really was going to occur that very year, but he had even narrowed down an exact block of time: during Rosh Hashanah.

As Richard explained excitedly in Sunday school that next week, he was at first doubtful. He had been looking into it for weeks before he made the decision that it was safe to share with us the imminence of our rescue. At first, he'd been "totally bummed out," as he still had a lot of unfinished business on this planet. There was his book of memoirs he had only just started to write; plus he was entered in a regional dart tournament in September. It wouldn't be such a big deal, but his buddy from the "establishment" down the street was going, too— and he was sure to give his heart to the Lord any day. And, he admitted glancing sheepishly at his wife, Dina, he had sort of been hoping for a Richard, Jr.

"But it's OK," he told us excitedly. "I think I have things figured out. I might not even have to skip Regionals."

Over the course of the hour, we listened with excitement as he went through Whisenant's book. The 88 reasons he presented involved a large number of dates between events from the Bible. There were also political events, all symbolically alluded to, but if interpreted in a certain way could be witnessed first-hand on CNN. The biggest among these was the 40-year anniversary of Israel having become a nation, an event which took place in 1948. The Bible said that the generation that saw Israel become a nation once again would see the return of the Messiah. "Even so, when you see these things happening, you know that the kingdom of God is near. I tell you the truth, this generation will certainly not pass away until all these things have happened."[2] As Whisenant pointed out, a generation in the Bible lasts 40 years. Which brought us to 1988.

But there were other events, too. The Biblical text points to all manner of natural disasters, nations rising against nations, famines, earthquakes, as well as the preaching of the gospel to the entire world as indicators of the end of days. We all were familiar with the earthquakes and famines. It was the era of "Feed the World" and "Save the Children." Sally Struthers was a household name. By the time Richard was done, we were all convinced that Gorbachev was the antichrist with that weird Omen mark on his head and that we were never going to have to set foot in school again. Everyone was buzzing with excitement. Everyone, that is, except for me.

What I felt was that my head might explode.

"Wow," I said quietly, when he finally took a breath. "So, you think he's right?"

"Who, Whisenant?" He chuckled to himself as if I had said something funny. He winked at his wife, sitting against the back wall. "He's a Bible college student." As if that explained everything.

---

2   *Luke 21:29-32

I blinked back at him. Scott, sitting next to me, cleared his throat. Scott had been actively involved over the previous year in trying to expose the symbols of all of the various organizations that were potential world powers. He had even just finished a presentation to one of his classes at the public school—complete with a slideshow—which laid the plan of the Illuminati wide open based on the pyramid with the eye on the one-dollar bill. This was right up his alley.

"No. I don't think he's right," blurted Richard.

Some air audibly escaped through my mouth. A low rumble of commentary started rolling through the room. One of the junior high boys squeaked.

"This guy thinks that the Rapture is going to happen at the beginning of the seven years of Tribulation." He flipped some of his hair back. Something akin to dread was rising deep within me.

"No, guys. That Whisenant fellow is a *pre-tribber*. I am a *mid-tribber*."

We continued to stare blankly at him.

"He's got good evidence that we're nearing the end of this earth, guys. But I'm afraid he's got one key thing wrong: the Rapture isn't going to happen until the *middle* of the Tribulation. Oh, no. [insert mirthless chuckle] Quite a lot is going to happen between now and then. We've got a good three and a half years to go."

Something in the pit of my stomach twanged. I had heard about the Tribulation. It was supposed to be a time of great trial for Christians. My Dad had read to me about the time when Catholics and Protestants were fond of taking turns burning one another, and I knew that a Tribulation could only be worse.

And then there was 666, the Mark of the Beast, which would be put on either the forehead or right hand. When I was a kid, I was not allowed to draw on the backs of my hands or even put a sticker there for fear that it might accidentally be the Mark of the Beast. And while I was never quite sure how a Care Bears sticker might possibly be mistaken for "the Mark," I was well drilled in what the ramifications would be should I one day awaken to its presence on my person. Basically, all those good feelings between God and me throughout my life would be forfeited and I would be left alone to eek out a hollow existence amongst the wicked.

I sat there on the floor for some time, taking big sips of air and trying to see through the rapidly closing tunnel of staticky blackness. Somebody who noticed my heaving chest handed me a Styrofoam cup of water, which I ended up spilling on the hand-off.

Richard, unable to ignore the little scene from the front made his way through the pressing odor of teen spirit and knelt down in front of me. I felt a hand on my shoulder and listened as if through a drive-thru speaker as he began a heartfelt prayer for me.

"Help us to accept what must come," he was imploring as I finally began to regain any measure of awareness of my surroundings. "Let us just trust in You, that You are in control."

The blackness had rescinded and my head had regained its former clarity. Wow. We were really going. I could hardly believe it. It was so...exciting. I felt it swell within me. I looked up into Richard's face, surprised at the progress of stubble and breath that smelled like stale TaB. His eyes, which bore the signs of a life spent in ministry among smokers, were squinted earnestly as he prayed. He must have realized I was watching him, because he stopped suddenly and opened his eyes. I watched as his mouth spread into a warm smile.

And that's when I saw it. The empty, drained look we'd been worried about was gone and had been replaced by something else. Suddenly, Richard's face looked healthy—vibrant even. As far as Richard was concerned, he was now dealing with the fate of the world. And I'd never seen him happier.

*

While the average person may occasionally enjoy getting goose bumps about the extinction of humankind, Evangelicals thrive on it. As in, they expect it. Pray for it. Indeed, the average Evangelical craves it. Why? Because it means that this temporary life will end and a real one will begin. One that is absent of pain, destruction or marginalization. All of the pleasures that got put off—all of the fun that was deferred—will be rewarded times ten. Any lost friends who were also believers will be returned. Families will be restored. It will be a life in which we can finally begin to truly live. It will be a life that is *real*.

But for all of its popularity, the concept of living in a temporary world careening toward destruction has had quite the opposite effect on me over the years. It makes me uneasy.

Please don't mistake me. It is not that I do not long for something more than the life that I have been given. It is not that I do not hope for a lovely afterlife. It is quite simply that the all-consuming concept of a temporal, unreal world is what made me lose sight of what is right in front of me. Because if the world I am living in is not exactly real or lasting and it is only the soul that matters…then why should I prioritize taking care of the physical world, or anyone in it?

Evangelicals claim approximately 34% of the US population, ahead of the Catholics at 25% and the mainline

Protestants at 18%. In other words, it's kind of a big community. It's so big, in fact, that today there are no less than 1,000 of the 38,000 Christian denominations that fall under the heading "Evangelical," worldwide. People have been busy since the time of Martin Luther.

And restless.

Why all of the restlessness? It would seem that anyone who has a different interpretation of the Bible feels the need to start a new sect. The old church "didn't have it right"? Well. Let's start a new one. One that's *right*. So much more right, in fact, that in the more fundamentalist denominations, many are under the impression that the other 37,999 Christian denominations have missed the mark so egregiously that they should probably not qualify as Christians at all and will be attending orientation day in Hell along with the rest of the heathens.

True, Evangelicals generally believe the same things regarding the virgin birth, the triune nature of God, and the necessity to be "born again" through belief in Jesus as the means to being rescued from Hell. But while uncertainty and/ or error in interpretation of the Bible is not an option, there are plenty of things to get riled up about aside from the basics. Does God choose who will be saved or can anyone be part of the club? Can people achieve a life without sin? Should people be immersed in water to be baptized or is sprinkling adequate? Should the church use the Apostles' Creed in its liturgy or should it avoid creeds—or liturgy, for that matter— altogether? And on and on.

And on.

The fact that there are so many Evangelicals with such a diverse background ought to be the first clue to people outside the church that it is not comprised solely of Jerry Falwell and

Pat Robertson disciples. Evangelical churches are fragmented across doctrinal and theological lines with more cracks and splinters than a century-old woodshed. In looking at a diagram of the splits and fusions over the years, it would seem that anybody with above average leadership qualities has taken it upon themselves to start their own church based on their interpretation of the Bible. To the outsider, it would appear that the Evangelical community is hugely and unwittingly divisive.

For a growing number of us who grew up in the church, we've had enough. A lot of us have left, while still others of us remain part of the church community—because we love the *community* and the *search* and what we know it should be— but quietly seethe over dogmatic opinions, a dumbing down of the intellect, and a rising emphasis on the entertainment value of the Sunday service as if it's an in-flight show as we zoom toward our destination.

Devangelicals are everywhere and we are not always easy to spot. Many have left the church altogether, while still others have not. This is because being a Devangelical is more a state of mind than it is about a choice of faith community.

While not every Devangelical has left the church as a result of this analysis, it is worth noting that according to a 2008 American Religious Identification Survey from Trinity College, the fastest growing religion in the US is "non-religion" (15% in 2008, up from 8% in 1990). True, not all of these are from the Evangelical church, but certainly the church is feeling the hit. Is it a sign of the Devil's grip, as some would claim? Or is there a valid reason behind the mass exodus? Is it that we've lost our faith, or are we fed up with the institution? Is it both?

All I can say is what happened to me.

The Power of Suggestion

As a teenager I loved my Youth Group. Every Wednesday night, no matter how much homework I had, Mom or Dad drove the 30 minutes across town to our church, where my younger sister and I were deposited, no questions asked. Two hours later, we would emerge rosy-faced, talking too loudly, and in need of another layer of deodorant.

Everybody in the church knows that it is the teenage years that are crucial if one is going to keep its flock on this side of the flames. Also, if you miss pulling in people in their adolescent years, it's anybody's guess if they'll stick around to be card-carrying members of the tithe paying adult congregation.

Thus was Youth Group paramount.

We would play our silly games like wall ball and *"how much baby food can you eat before you puke"* before gathering together in a splatter-painted room that I will call "The Lion's Den" to talk about God and how succumbing to the pressures of today's world will land you squarely in Hell. But if the avoidance of Hell via a lifetime church membership is the Prime Directive, then Starfleet General Order 2 for the existence of the Youth Group is to take the place of sex.

There's the foreplay. First, we would line up for games. Boys on one side, girls on the other. At first, it was all about the heart rate. We'd run races. We'd see who could skip the fastest, wrap ourselves in toilet paper the quickest, spin in circles for the longest. Slowly, things would progress. The boys would hoist the girls on their shoulders, the girls bearing handfuls of whipped cream.

It is here that our Youth Pastor gathers us together.

Pastor Mark is a gentle man, well-groomed hair, handsome. He is paid minute

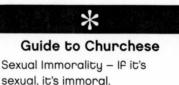

Guide to Churchese
Sexual Immorality — If it's sexual, it's immoral.

doses of US currency to keep our group of acne-spackled teens on the right side of the gates of the kingdom. He has eyes filled with compassion regardless of whether he is preaching the word of the Lord or pleading with the junior high kids to stop lighting farts in the stairwell. It hasn't been too long since he has graduated from college, so he knows what we're going through. He relates. For him, the struggle is over, having recently married his college sweetheart. *And believe me*, he tells us, *the wait is worth it*. We giggle in spite of ourselves. Some of us, jealous as hell, can't help but perspire a little at the thought. A few of us girls glance over at his wife feigning embarrassment at the back of the room.

We are impressed by their candor. We cannot help but be blown away by their realness. They are cool in spite of their years and if they were still in high school, we would totally be friends.

He stands at the front of us sweat-drenched, panting teenagers and tells us about a better way. The right way. Feeling hot for each other? Get hot for God instead! Need a cause to believe in? Get fired up for Christ! Be a radical Christian! Together, we have embarked on a journey. It has its ups and its downs. Jesus wants to love us fully. Completely. If only we would let Him! It doesn't matter what we've done in the past.

There are tears. We hug. We cuddle. We are invited to take it a step further and pray the prayer of repentance as we have done so many times in the past. Many of us do. If any of us want to go for ice cream down the street afterwards, we are invited along—a post-Youth Group activity fittingly called an *Afterglow*.

*

I lost my virginity thanks to a Youth Group outing and a group of impossibly large men.

OK, OK—not my real virginity. Being the good little Evangelical girl I was, I was saving that for my wedding night. But my spiritual virginity was as good as gone.

We hadn't exactly planned it. With my sights set on the End of the World, how could I have anticipated that there would be another ending waiting for me? How it managed to sneak up like that when we were trying to be so spiritual is beyond my comprehension. Scott and I attended Youth Group fanatically, attempting to fill the call of sexuality with spirituality as we had been taught. Sure, we had sneaked off to the back stairway a few times to make out, but we had always had our boundaries. I knew all too well that God didn't take half-assed boarders into His kingdom. Revelation 3:16 says, "But since you are like lukewarm water, neither hot nor cold, I will spit you out of my mouth." It was time more than ever to be hot. Scalding, even. I was going to be the ultimate follower. When God sat scrutinizing me from His throne on Judgment Day, I knew beyond a shadow of a doubt that He would welcome me into the kingdom with a grin and a high five because I was His kind of people.

Of course, all the usual suspects were there. Scott had that broad smile and those piercing green eyes. He was smart.

Funny. I was a self-consciously dressed, giggling mess who no longer had the time for any of my girlfriends. The sheer amount of dopamine cycling our systems every time we got together had to be bordering on toxic. But we had prayed about that. We had put God in control.

That fateful weekend, we boarded the Youth Group bus along with 30 or so other hormonal teens for a field trip. The bus, whose name was "GUS" for God's Ultimate Servant, had been our project the previous year. We'd had a pancake supper to raise enough funds to buy it second-hand, with the intention of being able to bus kids to church on Sunday who didn't have rides. Being the late 80s, we spent one whole Saturday throwing day-glo paint at it in an attempt to make it the coolest vehicle for Christ in all of Colorado Springs. Unfortunately, there were only one or two kids who actually needed a ride to church and there seemed to be a bit of a debate as to whether they were coming with their parents' permission or not. When the church board expressed concern about a potential lawsuit, its Sunday morning glory ride was retired soon after. But when it was field trip time, it was Gus's time to shine.

This wasn't just any field trip, mind you. We, along with half the city, were headed to the city arena where we would watch gape-jawed as muscle-encased men bent rebar with their teeth and broke blocks of fiery ice with their foreheads.

That's right, John Jacobs and the Power Team had come to our town. Boy, were we jazzed. Richard was equally stoked. He even wore his muscle shirt which read "Jesus!" across the front, where the middle "s" was in the shape of a lightning bolt just like Kiss used.

Our Youth Pastor and his wife were there, too, giddy as the rest of us. Beaming, Scott and I herded in with the crowd to take our seats in one of the balconies.

Over the course of the next two hours, we were awed by these modern-day Sampsons. There were seven of them. Huge, hulking men with a clear message for Christ in between acts of wonder—changing the world, one head-bashed brick at a time. It was like a circus, only not. A human version of a monster truck rally, only not. A behind the scenes peek at the hulks of WWF, only not. Whatever the case, it was strong, relatable, and completely cool. Only....

One of them would stand before us as John Jacobs announced:

"See this man? His name is Bo."

A giant of a male specimen appeared next to John Jacobs, his muscles quivering in the limelight like a Clydesdale's.

"He gave his heart to the Lord Jesus Christ eight years ago. Bo is no pansy, folks, he stands 6'5" and weighs in at 322 pounds. Don't be fooled by his massive exterior, he's a got a teddy bear heart."

The women in the audience raised up a collective giggle. I allowed myself to wonder whether he would find me attractive if we were stuck in an elevator together.

"Now you've already seen him crush through a wall of ice eight feet thick tonight. But that ain't nothin'. The thing about Bo is—*the crazy thing about Bo is*—he's got a set of lungs like you wouldn't believe. Now he's gonna take this water bottle, and he's gonna blow it up until it pops like a toy balloon."

We all watch in rapt attention as he dangles an ordinary hot water bottle before us, Shocked that a mere mortal can accomplish such an act, we burst into applause. I am feeling faint. I look over at Scott, who is glowing at me.

"Now this ain't no toy, heh heh. Just so you know that we're not playing any tricks on you tonight, I've invited an expert in the field to determine whether this is, in fact, a genuine hot water bottle. Grandma, can you come up here for a moment?"

We cheer as a frail looking woman approaches the stage. We are reverently amused at the contrast between grandmother and grandson. She speaks something crackly into the mike and we raise a mighty cheer. Bo stands before us now and puts his lips to the bottle. Guitars scream over the speaker system and a beat thumps through our skeletons.

"Now ladies and gentlemen," John tells us over the music as Bo begins to blow. "This is something Bo has done over 1,000 times. If he fails, a rush of air so strong will force its way back into his lungs, causing them to burst. Just because he's done it before does not ensure his success. Do not attempt this at home. Just one mistake, ladies and gentlemen. Just one mistake..."

The suspense builds as Bo blows into the hot water bottle. He hesitates a little and I hear someone behind us begging, "Please Jesus." Bo seems to get over his hump and deposits another lungful of air into the hot water bottle, now as big as a soccer ball. He's on a roll now. It's as big as a five gallon cooler. He *huff huff HUFFS* into the bottle until—POW! It explodes like a flimsy balloon! *Oh!* How great the strength-of-Jesus-metaphorically-speaking is! Scott grabs me around the shoulder and pulls me in for a victory squeeze. Oh yes! How great He is indeed!

Bo Who Can Blow diminishes during the applause to the back of the line-up just as another hulk of a man jogs up to the front. He has a phone book in his hands. Effortlessly, he *R-R-RIPS* it in two! The crowd erupts. But the men are just warming up. We have yet to witness John Jacobs, himself, snap the chains between not one, but TWO sets of handcuffs from his wrists. The music is cut off so that we can hear the sound of the chains as they tear. We know that what he does is by his own strength and that he is only demonstrating what Jesus does for us figuratively, but it doesn't matter. We are pretty sure Jesus has something to do with it. None of us can rip handcuffs from our wrists like origami Christmas chains. People around me cry out, "Jesus!" just before he does it. We hear the mighty snap. HE DOES IT! It's a MIRACLE! How we praise Jesus for breaking the chains that bound us after that! The crowd goes NUTS! I'm crying. Scott is screaming. People have their hands in the air to thank the Father above for these men who remind us of only a fraction of His power.

An altar call is initiated. The Power Team boasts that 2-3 out of every 10 people who show up to their performances give their lives to Christ—and I can see from my place in the balcony that it's at least that many. People are pouring down the aisles to give their lives to Christ—and perhaps to also touch the members of the Power Team. John Jacobs is there to lay his hands on foreheads and slap high fives. And it really is that amazing. People are changed. Some people claim to be healed. Many are saved.

*

In the years since my attendance that night, I have lived in several different places. Currently, I live in Boulder, Colorado—which everybody knows is 25 square miles surrounded by reality—and I'm not so sure that the Power Team would go over so well with this crowd. The people here are entirely too, I don't know, *metro* or something. The idea of testosterone-dripping, red meat-eating men (and now one woman) might be seen as an affront to our vegan-spirited little utopia here. Well, they might dig the chick, but that's not the point.

But we had seen just what we needed to see that night. Jesus truly isn't for sissies. He is strong. Indisputable. In control. Tough. Manly. Virile...

Back on the bus after a two-hour long adrenaline rush, we were exhausted. My friend Amy and her boyfriend Matt sat opposite us in the back seat of the bus, laughing privately about some inside joke. Some of the kids, still vibrating from the evening's performance, were loud at first, but quickly settled into a pattern of silence. One or two fell asleep. I fell into Scott's arms.

It was just a lot of kissing at first, I swear. We had been through a lot together that evening and we just felt so…close. So ooey-gooey, ishy-squishy close. At first, when he began touching me under my shirt, I was alarmed. But he just said, "Shhh, I think God has given us to each other." Well, that just about made my heart go crazy with desire. To think that God had preordained us to be together! We were special. *Radical.* And quite possibly in a league all of our own. Surely God would not judge us poorly. But it was OK. Nothing actually bad was happening. It wasn't the real deal, anyway. It was like something wrong…only not.

I did peek over at Amy and Matt once or twice, but they were too distracted to notice what was going down in the seat next to them. Or even in the seats all around them, for that matter. Because by the appearance of things on the Youth Group bus that night, Bo was not the only one who could blow.

Dancing with the Devil

Part of what allowed me to be happy about my own numbered days early on was that I did not belong to this world. Not really, anyway.

To the outside world, the Evangelical's brand of Christianity has come to be synonymous with "under educated, uncultured, over-reactive hypocrites who don't want anybody else to have any fun." And, Evangelicals, if this is the first time you're hearing what "the world" thinks of you, then I'm sorry to be the one breaking the news. But I think most Evangelicals know this, somehow.

I certainly knew it, and I wore the label with a sort of smug irony. The world simply didn't understand. I was certainly educated, exposed to culture, and was most definitely not a hypocrite. Any names they called me didn't matter in the slightest. I loved the chance to prove them wrong. Both of my parents had doctorate degrees and regularly took us to world-class symphonies and concerts. I had studied three languages in addition to my own, traveled outside the country numerous times in my youth, played several instruments, and read everything from Twain to Tolstoy. At home, my mother had taught me well about everything from correct posture by walking with a book on my head, to using the outside fork first, to "how to curtsy should you ever meet the Queen of England." And while we were not exactly wealthy by American standards, my parents made sure we had what we needed and, most importantly, that we carried ourselves as if we had far more. "The world" would be watching us, after all—judging us based on our beliefs and we had to show them that what we had…was better than what they had. We would win them to Christ through our thoughtfulness, our culture, and our intelligence.

Guide to Churchese

Christ-like Example – What people should be doing in response to the popular question WWJD (What Would Jesus Do?) so that people will see that we have the love of Christ in us and are holier than they are.

But even so, I was keenly aware that my "citizenship" was in Heaven, so what did it matter what mere earthlings called me? My sights were set beyond any of this fray. Far beyond. As far as I was concerned, Jesus was coming any day to take me home and then the people of the world would be sorry. Nobody would be laughing then. There would be no sarcastic snickers on the last day of the world.

Being 'in the world' and not 'of the world' is an important distinction to the Evangelical. God calls His people to be different, the argument goes. Set apart. I Peter 2:11-12 says, "Dear friends, I urge you, as foreigners and exiles, to abstain from sinful desires, which wage war against your soul. Live such good lives among the pagans that, though they accuse you of doing wrong, they may see your good deeds and glorify God on the day he visits us."

In other words, while it may have been important to love and hang out with my pagan friends at school, not everything they did was OK for me to take part in. I was supposed to be different. Or, in the words of famed God rockers, Petra: "We are strangers, we are aliens, we are not of this world."

So when it came to things that I knew I was not supposed to be doing, it gave me comfort to remind myself that I belonged somewhere else. I was a citizen of Heaven, after all—not California or Kansas or Oklahoma or Colorado or wherever my parents happened to have moved us.

So, what was I not supposed to be doing?

For starters, anything to do with sex outside of marriage. That was easy—more in theory than in practice, of course— but I was aware of the sex problem. The God I had learned about through my parents and church hated sex outside of marriage. And since all I really knew on that topic as a young teenager was that any TV show or song that had even a hint of a sexual reference was instantly shut off and frowned upon by my parents in my presence, my impression was that sex in general was frowned upon by God, too. Ephesians 5:3 says, "But among you there must not be even a hint of sexual immorality, or of any kind of impurity, or of greed, because these are improper for God's holy people." And there you had it. Sexual immorality. Not just an immoral *type* of sexual behavior—as in, perhaps certain sexual behavior that might be frowned upon, for example orgies or sex with a temple prostitute—but the immorality of sex. Sex *equaled* immorality. It was obvious...wasn't it?

Of course, sexual behavior was not the only thing that separated us true Bible-believing Christians from the world (or from other Christians who may not have been so accurate in their theology). There were other things, too. Things like lying, getting drunk on wine, stealing...the list goes on. As a protective measure, or perhaps as a way to have a higher success rate in delivering every woolly creature within one's flock to the golden gate, our particular denomination had a list of activities which it had called out as "sinful," in so-called accordance with the biblical text. This list included theft, lies, extramarital/premarital sexual relations, drinking alcohol, dancing, watching movies, smoking, murder, and foul language, among others. And if any of these activities were questioned as being truly sinful, all one had to do was to point out how any or all of those activities *led* to sinful behavior and who amongst us wanted to be subject to that kind of temptation?

Ever since I was a young child, I tried to set a Christ-like example at all times, even when there was no one around to see it. In the car and at home I limited my listening pleasure to Christian radio, and sometimes to an Oldies station I could pick up. Whenever there was a bad word in a song that I had no control over listening to, I would hum and hold my fingers to my ears so I would not accidentally hear it. The one thing I knew above all else was that I did not want to go to Hell.

But it would only be a matter of time before the tide of popular culture would threaten to pull me under. I think this all came to a head for me at a slumber party I really shouldn't have attended back in the seventh grade.

*

It was Bridget's idea. Since it was her birthday and her house, no one really felt like objecting. Not that anyone would have stood in her way, anyhow. She was *only* the most popular girl I have ever known. It would have been like Angelina Jolie inviting you to a party at her house and then you telling her that you didn't want to talk to her because she has too many tattoos.

I was already feeling guilty. Before I left home that night, I stopped in the kitchen to say goodbye to Mom before my father drove me to the slumber party. My mother has a style of her own. She has a Ph.D., speaks fluent German and French, and is a professional harpist. Having lived in both Austria and Iran for periods of her life, she had adopted a subtle international flair. Her real passion was in medieval studies, leading her sometimes to wear long, fluid dresses with empire waists while I was in my younger years.

Because of all of this international influence, she developed a rather eclectic palate early on and likes to experiment with food from different parts of the world. Back then it was always something that teenagers in the 1980s had never heard of, like hummus or mousaka. That evening, she was spooning polenta over a steaming bowl of ground meat and olives into something she calls a tamale pie. She paused to look me directly in the eye.

"Will there be a movie?"

I hesitated. I didn't think so.

"If they watch a movie, you call me and I will come get you. You have no business watching *that trash.*"

Now, while our particular denomination's handbook did clearly state that going to a movie theater was considered ungodly behavior—and therefore a sin—watching movies in the privacy of one's home was not on the no-no list, *per se.* For some time, I assumed that this was because bad things look even worse in a theater—that the large screen acts as a magnifying glass of sorts. What might be a casual kiss on a 19" Sony would reveal itself to be a full-fledged Grecian orgy on the silver screen. The cigarette dangling from Humphrey Bogart's mouth on our old black and white Zenith, when magnified 20 times, would no doubt prove to be nothing less than a crack pipe.

Eventually, I realized that the reason we were not allowed to watch a movie at the theaters had more to do with the actual theater itself. Horrible, perverse things happen there. Theaters are regular hangouts for unsupervised teens and escaped convicts. Practically everybody is either doing drugs or having sex in the darkened seats.

Even so, my mother had assumed that any movie we would be watching at Bridget's—no matter how small—would be filth. Bridget's parents, after all, did not go to our church and did not know the rules. By asking me to call-in-case-of-movie, she was only trying to protect me. But by the time popcorn had been popped, pajamas had been donned and *Breakin'* was pushed into the VCR, it was late and I felt really stupid calling my mom to come get me.

I was torn. Was I supposed to inform my peers that they were all going to Hell because they were watching a movie and I was going to call my mommy and tell? Bridget's parents certainly didn't seem to mind. Her father, who turned out to be just as cool as she was, even watched it with us and totally pulled off some of the rad breakdancing moves we saw on screen. And he was even an usher at their church.

Still deeply in the middle of being shocked and awed by my very first non-Disney, I barely even registered what was happening until later—until it was too late. I mean, it was *Breakin'*! It was a movie...and dancing...in one! I was so overloaded by the whole event that I hardly knew what to do with myself. If that was sinning, I liked it!

Later in the bathroom that night, I would stand in front of Bridget's sticker-framed mirror for at least five minutes trying to send a wave through my body from one set of fingertips to the other, just like Ozone and Turbo had done. I whispered the words: *"Push it to pop it! Rock it to lock it! Break it to make it!"* to my own reflection and tried to imagine what I would look like in Kelly's leotard. I didn't know how, but I knew then that I needed to buy parachute pants and a zipper jacket and move to the beach.

Anyhow, I was energized from the movie. Was it really wrong to be so excited about it? Surely my mother would be horrified if she knew about it.

My mother. I thought back to the time when a friend and I had watched Disney's *The Black Cauldron*. Just the name was enough to send her reeling forcibly backwards into the stuffed grape leaves she was making for dinner.

When I came out of the bathroom, I almost got knocked down by a couple of girls doing the worm across the family room floor. Somebody had put on DC Talk as loud as it would go, and the whole place had gone crazy. I looked over at Juliette, a friend from school. Juliette was beautiful. When the rest of us chose to spend hours in front of the mirror every morning maintaining an evenly curled and shellacked tidal wave, she wore her blonde hair smoothly side swept across her brow, giving her a naturally glamorous look. Juliette jumped up from the couch when she saw me and pulled me into the room past one girl attempting the sprinkler. In that environment, it wasn't too difficult to forget that I was a child of God.

"Watch this!" I told Juliette, and proceeded to demonstrate the wave I had been practicing. She doubled over with laughter and tried it, too. Pretty soon, Bridget's dad came back in the room and tried the Scramble, which he did a little *too* well. By the time Bridget stood before us all in her baseball uniform nightshirt and suggested we play Light as a Feather, I was already in too deep to turn back. *Breakin'* had already broken me.

Bridget's best friend, Nina, volunteered to go first—a relief to me since I was on my period and was self-conscious about the enormous maxi pads I had to wear. I was the only girl at the party who was wearing sweats under my otherwise perfectly normal nightgown. That is, if you consider it normal to wear a nightgown which hung down to the floor and had enough ruffles on it to make a 1970s prom king deliriously happy.

Nina was clearly a returning player to the game based on her knowledge of the lingo. She lay down willingly in the midst of us girls, looking down on her in our newfound enthusiasm for sinning as if we were about to sacrifice her to the White Witch. Nina's sister, Chris, sat beside her while Bridget took her head and encouraged the rest of us in a Siren voice to scoot closer and to stick two fingers between her body and the carpet.

When it was time to do the lifting, we all got eerily quiet and began chanting. At this point, I started to get scared that we were allowing ourselves to be vessels for Satan, so I only mouthed the words. Together we lifted Nina who was, indeed, stiff as a board. It was a bit of a debate when it was all over, however, whether she had truly been as light as a feather, which ended up sending her off in a flurry of tears to the bathroom where she would be consoled for the next hour by Chris. The rest of us raided the kitchen for processed substances.

Which was right about the time when Bridget waltzed in with a Ouija Board and a saccharine smile.

"Nina's fine," she shrugged, tossing her perfect, dark and curly hair over her equally perfect shoulders. "Let's play this instead."

My eyes grew as big as stoplights and I turned to Juliette, who was in the middle of dissecting an Oreo with her newly forked tongue. She was still kind of sweaty from our illegal dancing session and a strand of long hair stuck seductively sideways across her forehead. Even Bridget's natural curls couldn't compare. I leveled my eyes at her and spoke firmly.

"We can't play that."

Juliette just rolled her eyes at me and took a slurp of milk.
"Why not?"

"Because it's *totally* Satanic! I heard that they have a witch at
Milton Bradley put a curse on each and every game."

Sometimes I wondered about Juliette. How could she not
know these things? We may have gone to the same school, but
we obviously came from different worlds. She went to a fairly
conservative church, too, so I know she should have known
better. I mean, I didn't even have a Speak 'N Spell when I was
little because it sounded like the Devil and had the word 'spell'
in it. Clearly, her parents had given her too much latitude. I
softened my tone and even managed an understanding smile.

"Milton Bradley has a witch on their payroll?" Juliette
asked me, raising one eyebrow. Her father was some big
business executive and she was always coming out with this
kind of thing. I wasn't sure I even really knew what a payroll
was.

"Yes, Juliette, they do."

She tossed me a cookie.

"We should French braid your hair tonight."

And I thought she had forgotten. We made our way over
to the couch so she could work her magic on my hair. We got
to laughing and talking in our own little world, so when a girl
named Debbie came in crying and hugging her shoulders, we
needed to be brought up to speed. She pointed into the next
room where the girls were playing with the Ouija Board.

"It just told me that somebody in my family is going to
die. I don't want anybody in my fam-nghee da dy-eee!" she
finished off with a nearly unintelligible squeak.

Juliette looked at her with her signature one-eyebrow
raise.

"Debbie, of course somebody in your family is going to
die. Everyone in your family is going to die."

"Juliette!" I snapped when Debbie started gushing snot into my shoulder.

"Sorry! But everyone dies eventually. That's all I meant. I don't mean they're all going to die next week."

We followed her into Bridget's room where everyone was huddled together on the floor on the other side of Bridget's bed. The lights were out and nobody was talking. Just then Bridget exploded.

"Aw, man! Why won't it tell me who I'm going to marry? Nina, you should ask it. I'll bet it's going to tell you that you're going to marry Jason—and that you'll have seven kids."

Horrified, I watched from the doorway as Nina placed her hands on the pointer and it started to spell out J-A.... I couldn't watch anymore. Clearly, there was a demon in Bridget's own bedroom and she didn't even recognize it. I looked around her room decorated in hot pink with black stars, which were only mere circles away from being pentagrams, and wondered where it was hiding. Would it go away when we stopped playing the game, or would it linger under the dust ruffle somewhere? An image came to me of a witch dressed in black from her tall, pointy hat to her toes standing in the manufacturing aisle at Milton Bradley and cackling her head off. I cursed her in my heart.

I clutched Juliette by the arm. I had to get out of there. Dragging her behind me like a hostage into the hallway, I stopped to take a breath against the wall—just as Jenn, Bridget's little sister, came into view.

Jenn was in the same grade as my little sister and had even come to our house once or twice for birthday parties. I hadn't noticed her at the party earlier or in the hallway before, standing up against the partially open hall closet door. But there she was, heart heavy with accusations and eyes filled with tears.

"I'm telling," she whispered unsteadily to Juliette and me. My mind snapped back to earlier in the evening, and my breath caught.

"It was just the wave," I told her, my knees feeling suddenly like they might give out. She glared back at me as if I had just killed her entire family with a pickaxe. Then, quick as lightning, she made a break for it down the hall.

With my back to the wall, I thought through the events of the evening, trying to connect the three into a series of steps that led from one to the other. Had the dancing opened the possibility for Light as a Feather, which in turn, had led to the Ouija board? Or had it been the presence of the Ouija board that had influenced the dancing? Or was the Ouija board and Light as a Feather in a class of their own and the dancing…was just fun? Was it wrong of me to think so?

I was getting confused. I loved God. More than anything, I was overwhelmed by awe when I thought of how enormous a being would have to be to have created all of us and then to manage our complexity. And when I thought of how even through all of that, that being wanted the best for me, all I could feel was grateful. From everything I had been taught, I felt like I almost knew Him, too. No, that wasn't right—I *did* know Him. Of course I did. Wasn't that the question preachers asked Sunday after Sunday: "Do you know Him?" And the correct answer was "Yes!" To not know Him had some pretty dire consequences. He was the one who gave me those powerful feelings when I was in a particularly emotional service…or when I lay on my back in the grassy backyard and closed my eyes with my face to the sky. Sure, I had danced. I had popped and I had locked. My feelings for God had not changed. Had His changed for me? Did God look at me different now?

FREEBIRD

I HAVE BEEN A "YOUTH GROUPIE" IN A VARIETY OF CHURCHES under the Evangelical umbrella. My involvement in this particular denomination—which shall remain unnamed here—was my idea; not my parents'. While it is true that I had been born into this denomination, my family had branched out before my insistence on a return to the firmly supported bosom of fundamentalism.

Today's Evangelicals come from a long line of folks who are disenchanted with the current system. It is a proud history with roots as far back as the Anglican church, which broke from Rome in the mid-1200s. From there, it has spun off denominations and movements faster than a Water Wiggle. Our particular denomination branched off the Arminian Holiness Movement, which in turn branched off the Methodists. While we weren't inclined to cut loose dancing and spouting tongues in church like the Pentecostals, we were handshaking cousins with loud and firm affirmations shouted from the pews and at least one hand raised in the air during praise choruses.

First had been a transfer to the Quaker church for a couple of years. It was here that I learned to sit still through endless minutes of prayerful silence while beads of sweat dripped from my temples as I forbade myself to scratch at the places where my tights met the wooden pew. To this day I associate the picture of William Penn on the Quaker Oats cylinder with the flames of Hell and an itchy perineum.

Immediately before I ever stepped foot in The Lions Den, I was active in a downtown Presbyterian church, renowned for its high society parishioners and Calvinist leanings. My parents had started taking us there primarily because my father's job seemed to demand it. Having recently become a vice president in a well-known Christian foundation for high school kids, he quite simply needed to be in a place where he could mix and mingle with the leaders in the community. And despite the fact that I used to spend most of the sermon spelling out the church bulletin in the sign language alphabet, even I could see that the pastor there really was quite eloquent.

After church I would stand with my younger sister—and sometimes my older half-sister when she was visiting—as if on display while we received a series of handshakes and cheek pinches from friends of our parents who smelled of fancy perfume and coffee breath. Having just moved from Oklahoma City, we were relatively new in town. Even so, the people at that church had accepted us warmly. Already, our family had moved states several times in my young life, so it meant a lot to have that sense of place—of home.

We probably would have stayed at the downtown church longer than we did if it were not for one little snag. At the time, a hundred or so of us teens met regularly in a large, dark wooden floored room with a balcony and rafters, from which I distinctly remember swinging like a monkey. The Youth Pastor there was a short, thickly mustached man who fulfilled the requirement of coolness in spite of the fact that he wore socks with his sandals. He would play loud music over the speakers while we all raced around in some sort of semi-controlled frenzy for half an hour before summoning us over for the weekly lesson. Being pre-Richard, I was pretty much convinced that he was the coolest Youth Pastor I had had thus far, until one night he did it.

"Why don't you guys come over here and settle down," he said amidst a bunch of titters and giggles from his adoring group. "I mean, *my God!*" And as if that weren't enough, he repeated what he had said. "*My God*, you guys are out of control!"

Amongst my peers, there was more laughter, but for me it was as if a needle had just screeched across a record. How could a Youth Pastor take the name of the Lord in vain? Wasn't that one of the Ten Commandments? I was stupefied.

> ✻
> ### Guide to Churchese
> Youth Pastor – A special sort of person with a tolerance for noise exceeding that of the average human—most likely due to a God rock phase which may or may not have run its full course. These gifted individuals lead the Youth Group regularly in songs and in some kind of peppy sermon and are considered "cool" by their teenage followers, despite the mandatory age gap and the propensity to make poor clothing choices. It is widely believed by the parents that this person is "in charge."

Granted, I had not always been a saint as far as language was concerned. That is to say, while at the time I had a mouth clean enough for a Mentos commercial, I had gone through a rough patch. It all started in the fourth grade when I was going with a boy at school who could swear anyone under the table and down into the cellar. Once, when my dad discovered that I was hanging out with this kid, he loudly maintained that if he ever caught him near me again, he would "kick him around the block a few times."

Dad was fond of sketching the various steps of our lives with an ink pen he kept on the inside of his suit jacket, and proceeded to draw a cartoon drawing of him dropkicking my boyfriend onto a giant boot.

In spite of the effective graphic demonstration, however, I continued "going with him," which mostly involved awkwardly sitting together in the lunch room and once kissing him in front of 30 or so chanting fourth graders yelling, "Kiss him! Kiss him!" For despite the fact that I was quite certain that foul language was a sin, I was also aware that it was fun. And it got attention. Unfortunately, it got the wrong sort of attention when a group of my church peers with whom I went to school ran an intervention on me in the girls' bathroom to let me know how much they were concerned about me and my filthy mouth.

"We're just worried about you," they told me. There were three of them, all huddled around me as if ready to perform an exorcism. "We don't want you to go to Hell."

My eyes darted to the floor as shame crept up my neck and cheeks.

"Jesus doesn't like it when we cuss," one of them whispered, squeezing my arm.

"When we cuss it's like we crucify Him all over again," added another.

Well, I straightened up after that. Found Jesus and asked Him to help me never ever say those words again. They were bad. Messed up. An outward expression of an inward condition.

That was it, really—the moment I accepted redemption and became born again. While I always wished I had a more impressive testimony—some amazing flash of light to which I could point, I'm afraid that was it. I was never strung out on drugs like Anne Lamotte or in prison like Chuck Colson. I was more like Stan on South Park—just a potty-mouthed kid who hung out with an even bigger potty-mouthed kid.

Even so, I took my new understanding of life very seriously. The one thing I knew above all else was that I did not want to go to Hell. What was more, I did not want my friends to go there either. If this meant curbing my bad language habit so that I could be a more effective witness, then so be it. So when a few years later my very own Youth Leader took the name of the Lord in vain, I broke up with him in my heart. Drop-kicked him on that proverbial boot.

Unfortunately, I discovered rather quickly that as I was not yet of age to operate a motor vehicle, I was stuck with my Youth Group. I could hardly redirect my entire family to a different church. My younger sister was actively involved in her group— as were my parents. So, quietly—patiently—I waited. I looked for any chance of breaking free from the confines of my Youth Group. So when my smut-mouthed Youth Pastor suggested we all go on a field trip to see Christian rocker, Rick Cua, I was in.

It being my first Christian rock concert, I was unleashed by the excitement. My friends and I ran a path between our seats and the snack bar, riding a high of refined sugar and pure rock n' roll bliss. It didn't even matter that I wasn't that into the Christian metal scene—or "God rock," as it is often called. It was cool. It made me feel things I had never felt before. Things like uncontrollable giggles and the inexplicable urge to scream. Born again or not—had it been requested of me, I would have totally shown my boobs.

We had caught sight of some friends standing up next to the stage at one point and had been so thrilled that we spent the next ten minutes shouting, trying to get their attention.

When intermission came, we couldn't shut off. We were so full of energy that we literally ran circles in the girls' room, as if our feet didn't know how to stop moving. When the music started up again, we grabbed onto each other, running like a human ram through anyone in our path. This time, we would blast through the superfluous onlookers and procure standing room next to the stage, too. This time, we would not be denied.

After some effort, we made it up to the front. Rick Cua himself loomed above us playing his guitar like he'd made a deal with the Devil. Only he hadn't of course. For several minutes, I stood star struck. It didn't matter one bit that I had never heard of Rick Cua before. The dude could rock.

At some point, I felt a tap on my shoulder. Expecting it to be someone from my Youth Group, I turned around with a smile. But instead of a face, I met a chest. Readjusting my angle, I saw a tall, blond boy looking down at me. At 5'3", most people seem tall to me. But this boy stood at about six and a half feet. Something in the back of my throat caught and I stared at him like a deer caught in headlights. He was doing the same.

"Do I know you?" I asked when I could speak again. He smiled. Recognition spread over my face like sunrise. "Scott?" I asked.

I couldn't believe it. Scott had been in my fifth grade Sunday school class several years before when we had lived in Oklahoma. Was it possible that he had moved, too? He confirmed this, explaining how his family had coincidentally moved the exact summer mine had. We had been living in the same city for about six months now—without even knowing it.

I hardly recognized him. The last time I saw him, he was standing in the corner so petrified to talk to anybody, that he flushed lava lamp red if anybody walked within a five foot radius of him. There had been one time in Oklahoma when I felt so sorry for him that I gathered up a group of girls to go talk to him. He had been so mortified, that he could barely lift his eyes from his own feet. The boy standing before me now talked coolly and easily to me. He did not even so much as hint at needing to consult his feet for reference. And, he was cute.

"You here with your Youth Group?" he beamed, looking around at the concert that I had now all but forgotten.

"Yeah, but you know. Where do you go?"

He explained that he went to a church on the other side of town. If I wanted, I could ride with him sometime to check it out.

The rest of the concert flew by. All I could think about from that point on was that I had an out. It was the last event I would attend with my former Youth Group. Rock n' roll had freed my soul and I had a ride outta there.

*

Even after my return to extreme fundamentalism, I continued to dabble. Exposed to more than 60 denominations at my Christian school, I was insatiably curious. Over the years, I flirted with rebellion by spending time at the Bible Fellowship Church as well as a charismatic church or two, the most notable of which was New Life under Pastor Ted Haggard.

While I was busy blowing in the wind between denominations, something unexpected was taking root inside of me: a belief in both the goodness and the ugliness of humanity wherever I was. No one group had the answers; no one group was perfect. To believe so, I was quickly learning, was a delusion.

FOR THE SAKE OF THE CALL

THE DEVIL WAS A REAL PART OF MY EVERY MOVE AND thought. He hid in the corner of my room. His minions—*demons*—actively took part in trying to sway my every move. Cheat on that test. Listen to Madonna.

I believe a significant shift happened in the minds of young Evangelicals of my generation. Whereas the older generations believed that demons and angels existed and fought for spiritual ground, my generation believed that demons and angels fought over the pebbles. Every single thought or movement we could potentially make in a day was being watched over and influenced. If we lost our keys in the morning, it was a demon of confusion trying to make us question a God who would throw such stumbling blocks in our path. When we found the keys later that afternoon, an angel had cleared the path and led us to them.

Much of this can be traced to theologians from the last century, such as Francis Schaeffer, who brought imagery of the spiritual realms front and center for the Christian community. As for popularizing the idea of spiritual warfare in your own living room, though, a book by author Frank Peretti called *This Present Darkness*, followed by the sequel *Piercing the Darkness*, played an undeniable role. The title of the book is taken from Ephesians 6:12: "For our struggle is not against enemies of blood and flesh, but against the rulers, against the authorities, against the cosmic powers of this present darkness, against the spiritual forces of evil in the heavenly places." Few books written in that era would prove to be more influential on the Evangelical community.

The book itself is about a couple of newspaper employees who were uncovering a large plot to take over their town by a New Age group called The Universal Consciousness Society. Eventually, they meet up with a local pastor in prison, compare notes, and

✳ Guide to Churchese

Evangelism – The act of letting everyone around you know your spiritual stance so that they will be dazzled by your certainty enough to also decide to believe as you do, thus gaining the reward of eternal life for all involved.

figure out the gravity of what's going down. Throughout the story, angels and demons are seen fluttering in rafters and contributing to the narrative by allowing the reader to learn of the plot from their point of view. Once the "Good Guys" figure out what is happening, they fight back the "Bad Guys" and the town is once again restored to spiritual safety.

This fictionalized suggestion of the involvement of spiritual beings in the lives of the average Jack and Jane made an impression, to say the least. When *This Present Darkness* hit the shelves, it was an instant success, selling over 2.5 million copies by last count. Never before had the spiritual struggle been so vividly popularized in the minds of American Christians. It became our new reality. Our obsession. Everything we did centered on spiritual warfare. The Devil was fighting to take as many souls from God as possible and it was our job to stop him.

*

I have always asked a lot of questions. Why would God send people who had never heard of Jesus to Hell? When was Hell founded if it never appeared in the Old Testament? Why did Paul never mention it? Why did theologians insist on translating a trash dump outside of Jerusalem named "Gehenna" as "Hell" in the Bible?

When I voiced these questions at church, people told me— with the best of intentions, of course—that while questions were good, they would pray that the Devil would stop throwing a web of confusion on me. The church told me that I was born bad. Evil, even. It was Christ through me that made me a good person. The fact that I was having questions at all was simply evidence that my naughty self had not given everything over to him.

In other words, questions were bad.

And so, I went boldly forward. So when Richard asked if I wanted to go on a special project with him, I was all over it.

I listened apprehensively as he explained what was going down over the phone. That weekend, unbeknownst to the vast majority of the city, the various members and proponents of The New Age Movement were meeting. While the good Christian citizens of Colorado Springs stayed at home to balance their checkbooks, all manner of Wiccans, warlocks, and openly practicing Satanists were having something called a "Metaphysical Fair" in the city arena. Boy, were they in for a surprise.

Some kids rebel by doing drugs. Others rebel by dyeing their hair pink or by becoming punk rockers. Me? I rebelled by giving myself 100% to Jesus.

A subculture within Generation X, we weren't put off by people deriding us for our beliefs, we were ready to shout it from the rooftops, "Jesus doesn't make freaks out of people, he makes people out of freaks!" And with that battle cry, we were prepared to go to some extraordinary lengths. The New Agers were trying to take over our town, and we were going to take it back. Kind of a righteous reclamation, if you will.

Being in Colorado Springs, we were surrounded by hundreds of churches preaching much the same thing. It was the 1980s, pre-invasion of Focus on the Family, but the general city culture was headed in that direction with The Navigators and Young Life already firmly ensconced. As Coloradans nestled in the shadow of Pike's Peak, we loved the outdoors and God. People who didn't fit that mold were generally thought of as New Agers or just ignorant. And it was our mission to educate them.

"We'll meet in the church parking lot. We can take my car. Come early, and don't look too clean," Richard said.

After I hung up with him, I explained the situation to my parents. Mom was hesitant to let me go into what she called "that bizarre venue," but Dad's enthusiasm in combination with the promise that I would report fully on what I saw got me through. They made me promise to call home around lunch-time from wherever I was, not to make eye contact with anybody out the window of Richard's car, and not to listen to a single thing any of the heathens told me. Especially the Wiccans. As Dad explained with an unsettling glint in his eye, the Wiccans regarded themselves to be white witches. Neo-pagans. I knew that to carry on a conversation with them was just asking for a demon to whisper into my ear.

Not that having a demon whisper into my ear was, in itself, to be feared. To us, spiritual warfare was a daily reality. Demons whispered into ears all of the time. Told us all sorts of things. Things like, "Come on—you know you need to listen to Madonna."

But we had angels for that.

Unrelenting angels on guard 24/7/365. And not just one. Despite popular theology, having one angel which you can call your own is hardly biblical. Nowhere in the Bible does it say anything about having one specific angel assigned to you to get you through this life. Everyone in my church knew there are legions of angels!

And it's not like anybody can say just how many there are in a room at any given time. God threw one third of the angels to the earth along with Lucifer, which leaves two thirds on His team. That means, technically, that there are two good angels to every bad one. Where they cluster is anybody's guess. Maybe they like churches, maybe they don't. The point is, a person just can't assume that an angel is going to be around the next time a demon sneaks up and starts whispering. And that's where prayer comes in.

Everybody in the church knows that angels are fueled by premium, Grade-A prayer. If you need God's protection, you have to ask for it. And you have to get specific. None of this "watch over us" crap. If you want a little heavenly bodyguard action, you've got to ask that God will send a posse of armed angels to surround you and form a holy shield in the face of evil on June 14th at precisely 9:32 a.m. They've got to be a crack team of highly trained professionals with specializations in combat and swordplay. They've got to be the Marines of the Angelic Forces. But if you want them, you've got to ask for them. Which is exactly what we did in the church parking lot while leaning on the hood of Richard's Hyundai.

"Father," began Richard after several moments of worshipful silence. I joined hands with Christine, our reigning Bible Quiz Team champion and a quiet boy named Ben who I didn't know very well to form a circle with Richard. "We just pray for your protection today. As You know, we're about to enter a den of vipers. Witches. Warlocks. The boudoir of the Whore of Babylon, herself. We pray that You just send with us today a legion of Your best angels. Just surround us with Your army of light and peace. Allow us with Your Sword, which is Your Word, Father, to just fight back this dark army. Just send them screaming from our city. Tearing from our town. Crying in agony whilst in continuous, wretched torment, gasping for breath, submerged wide-eyed and desperate beneath the white-hot surface of the hideous lake of fiery doom until their tainted flesh shrivels into ash from their bones. In Your name, oh Mighty Prince of Peace, Amen."

Having parked the Hyundai under a "Not Responsible for Vandalism" sign in the giant parking lot, we sized up our mark. Before us loomed the city arena and, just as Richard had promised, the place was crawling with sin. I watched with a shudder as two men dressed in black, hooded capes walked toward the doors.

"Well, soldiers, this is it," said Richard. "This is what we've been training for. Now, I don't want to see anybody do anything stupid and blow our cover in there. No casualties. We're basically gonna spend one hour in there and then meet back at the front doors, at..." he glanced at his camo Swatch, "...eleven hundred hours. Any questions?"

We looked back and forth at each other, our faces stern with responsibility. Everybody had done as instructed and dressed for warfare. Ben had worn his short curly brown hair slicked back with product. Christine had worn red. Always dressed for combat anyway, Richard was sporting an acid washed polo-gone-muscle-shirt with a finely starched collar over a pair of military issue cut-offs. He looked good. The only way you could tell he was a Christian was if you happened to catch sight of the gold, dangly cross earring in his left ear though the shimmering coif.

I wasn't quite as sure about my attire. I'd carefully picked through my thrift store rejects the night before and had settled on a predominantly black ensemble, which I had been too nervous about to wear to school, but which I'd purchased due to a brand name craze for which I am not proud. I even scratched on some black eyeliner that I found in my mom's old makeup pouch that clearly hadn't been used for a while. It was so old and dry that I was afraid I had given myself a tattoo. I even bled a little during the application. Years later, when I actually did acquire a tattoo—an outward sign of my inward fall from grace, I've been told—I would think back to that moment as a sort of initiation.

We threw our hands into the center of our circle in front of the Hyundai and made a quick break. *For His Glory! Boo-yah!* Moments later, we found ourselves on the other side of the doors. Across the River Styx, as it were.

It was worse than I thought. The entire floor of the arena was filled with sin. For as far as the eye could see, there was booth after booth selling the Devil's wares: meditation books, crystals, dragon sculptures, smoking devices—it was endless. And then there were the booths offering the Devil's services: reflexology, fortune telling…massage.

One that caught my eye immediately was a large booth, around which were set up a few padded tables. People were lying on them with strange rocks down the middle of their bodies. One Shaman-looking man wearing purple suede pants and a black tank top was waving incense over them with a feather. The sign read: Chakra alignment/Energy work/Reiki. I had no idea what that meant, nor did I care to. Whatever it was, it was something of the Devil—of that much I was sure. I wanted to shake the people awake from their apparent trances, topple the rocks off of them, scream at them, "Don't you know you're being POSSESSED?" Instead, I held my tongue and milled along with the crowd, still—thankfully—undercover.

And that's when it hit me. I wasn't exactly sure what we were undercover for. I glanced to my left and to my right. Christine and Ben appeared to be taking everything in at about the same speed I was. A woman dressed in layers of skirts and scarves and who looked suspiciously like Stevie Nicks came rushing past us, laughing, and bumping me forwards as she brushed by. Some guy dressed in one of those black robes I had seen earlier soon followed, clearly herding her into an orgy scenario. I grabbed both Ben and Christine's arms on either side of me lest I be pulled in with them.

"Why are we here again?" I asked.

"What?" they yelled back in unison. The place was so full of noise, laughter—Stevie Nicks cackles—that they couldn't hear me. I made inadvertent eye contact with a woman with a bony nose who had unnaturally long fingers and was playing a hammered dulcimer. Quickly, I looked away. I had never met one before, but I was just sure she was a Wiccan. If I looked too long, she would see into my soul. Figure out why we were there. Her pet demons would tell her.

But why *were* we there? I looked frantically for King Richard, but he had disappeared. I thought back to his prayer. He had asked God to help us to "just fight back this dark army. Just send them screaming from our city. Tearing from our town." But how were we supposed to accomplish said act? And furthermore, how was the word "just" involved in any of this? As if turning a demon's soul into black ash...*was just a small matter.*

"What are we supposed to do?" I yelled again, once I'd pulled them into a brief huddle.

Christine cleared her throat.

"Go into all the world and preach the good news to all creation. Mark 16:15."

I blinked back at her. Her bright red sweater dipped dangerously into a lowercase 'v' over her chest for the occasion. Her long, auburn hair—which she normally wore in a ponytail in the back—had been moved coquettishly to one side.

I wished I had thought of that.

"We're supposed to preach...*to the Wiccans*?" These were Wiccans, right?

She shrugged.

"It says 'to all creation.'"

"I think Christine's right. Let's just talk to people about God." Ben put a hand on my shoulder and squeezed it meaningfully.

"What about blowing our cover?"

"Relax. God will keep us safe."

I was confused, but looking back and forth at my peers, it was clear that they were eager to do battle that day. I listened as they hatched a plan. Since Christine knew the Word so well, she would go off on her own. Talk to the locals. Blend. Ben would go with me. I thought I saw them exchange glances.

With Christine gone, I took control and led Ben to the nearest booth, determined to prove myself. Next to Ben and Christine, it was easy to feel inadequate. But I was determined to make a dent in the Lord's work that day. Of course, I still didn't know what that work entailed.

I leaned over the booth, terrified of what I might find and to whom I might be forced to talk. To my relief, there was a relatively quiet looking heathen manning the booth I had chosen. He was sitting in a folding chair, reading. I ran my fingers over a book that bore the symbol of a rose and a cross at the bottom and pretended to look fascinated. I knew I had seen that symbol before—in one of Dad's books, no doubt. Always interested in the Devil's creativity as far as other religions were concerned, my father had a rather extensive library on other religions. He had one entire bookcase dedicated to what he called "the abomination of Mormonism," alone. As if yanked to life by the Master of Puppets, the man behind the booth leapt to his feet.

"Ah," he said, waving his hand vaguely at me like a Jedi knight. "You're looking for your inner source. Compassion, strength, love—it's all there. Right inside of you."

Just then a woman entered the booth behind him—part of the army of Stevie Nicks clones—and gave his shoulders a meaningful squeeze. Like nearly every other woman in the place, she wore a multi-layered skirt with a see-through, ruffled top. Hers was purple.

She smiled at me over his shoulder and I looked away.

"So...do you believe in Jesus?" asked Ben, sparing no words. I fought feelings of shame and inadequacy. Why couldn't I be so frank? The man flicked his mind control hand at Ben.

"We're of the Rosicrucian Order. We've been around a lot longer than a lot of these other groups in here. Have a look." He fanned the hand of intrigue over his books like an unholy Vanna White. "I think you'll see great fodder for social reform."

"But, do you believe in God?" persisted Ben.

"Sure we do. Just perhaps not in the traditional Judeo-Christian sense."

"Don't you listen to a thing he says," a strange voice hissed in my ear. Something about the quality of the voice made me nearly jump out of my skin. I clamped my eyelids shut and tried to block it out. Although I knew it was a likely event that a demon would try to talk to me, I didn't think it would actually happen.

"I'm serious. Don't listen to a single thing. They have their so-called 'Adepts'. Not like the *real* Ascended Masters."

I cast a glance over at Ben who was still warming up the Rosicrucian for his imminent salvation. He didn't seem to be registering the demonic voice. Even I had to admit that it was not what I would have expected. I had listened to a lot of Carmen, and the voice wasn't anything like that. No, it was lighter. Higher. Kind of like it had sucked on a helium balloon before it started chipping away at my cochlea. Chattier, too.

Slowly, I turned to look. My eyes skimmed right over him at first. If it wasn't for his tightly curled red hair, I might have missed him altogether. My eyes readjusted to about chest level, focused on a pair of bright green eyes, red goatee, disproportionately large ears. Scanning quickly downward, I also noticed he happened to be wearing silver lamé bellbottoms over a pair of platform cowboy boots.

I was instantly furious. I mean, seriously. Was this munchkin demon some kind of a joke? A spiritual guffaw? Everyone knew demons were big with wings and smelled of sulfur. Were the angels...playing a trick on me? Was this a test? I stared hard at him.

"Hey," he said, leaning up secretively toward my ear. "I know something they don't."

"What," I dead-panned.

"We're being watched."

"No kidding," I said dryly.

"They're already amongst us. From up there." Slowly he tipped his head back and looked up at the ceiling so that his goatee pointed accusingly at me.

"Only it's not funny," I asserted, more to the angels than to him.

His clear green eyes snapped back to mine.

"Oh, no. Not funny indeed. Although, most people out there don't get that yet. They think it's one big joke. But they'll see. When the aliens come, they won't be prepared. But you and me, we'll know." He nudged me then and winked.

"We'll know what?" came Ben's voice at my side. Apparently he'd dead-ended with the Rosicrucian. I watched Ben's face, realizing that he was seeing what I was seeing.

"How to attract them."

"Who?" asked Ben.

"The aliens. Look, I've been on a space ship 27 times now, so I know. I have a special place I go in the forest. Concentrate all of my thoughts and create a spectacular flashing light with my forehead. That's when they come."

"Fascinating," said Ben.

"You mean, you're for real?" I asked, stupidly.

The little man wrinkled up his nose at me.

"What do you mean am I for real? Are you mocking me? You're mocking me." He looked genuinely hurt.

"I'm sorry. I didn't mean —"

"Whatever," he said, throwing his hands at me, his goatee turned off to the side, his heels clomping as he stormed away.

"What was that about?" asked Ben. I was just about to explain to him that I had thought the little man was a Lollipop Kid demon sent on a bet by some of the off-duty angels to test me when King Richard came running back. His hair was slicked back with worry and his gold cross glinted openly in the fluorescents.

"All right team, we should go. Stat."

"What's going on?" asked Ben, automatically giving his shirt a little tuck-in.

"It's Christine. I found her over at the 'Photo Your Aura' booth. Apparently she'd had hers done. Paid the five dollars in silver."

"What are you talking about?" I asked, incredulously. I had never heard of an aura before—let alone realized that a photo could be taken of one.

"Eye witnesses say she got the photo taken—and when she got it back, she wigged out. Then she started to quote the entire book of Deuteronomy. I grabbed her just as she got to the part about not shaving your forelocks. But we gotta go now. She's waiting for us by the door."

"Wow," whistled Ben.

I nodded in agreement. I had no idea she could quote the entire book of Deuteronomy.

We bolted as fast as we could out of there. It was just a small casualty. Nothing major. Christine would recover and we could try again. But just for a moment as we scrambled toward the Hyundai, I thought I had seen the most beautiful sight I would ever see: the children of God, working together—for the sake of the call.

LATE

IF I COULD SMOOSH EVERY SERMON I'VE EVER HEARD together and then divide by subject, the largest portion hands down would be about the salvation of the soul. Saving one's own soul and those of others is paramount in the Evangelical church. Sure, I've heard much on social issues as well, mostly in the context of "fruits." The idea here is that if a person has given his or her heart to the Lord, then their fruit will be that they help others.

While other people were emptying their bank accounts, believing that they wouldn't need money after Rosh Hashanah 1988, I registered at the public school. I had been attending a Christian school for the previous two years, and had a bad feeling about it. I felt I was getting soft. Jesus didn't separate himself from the sinners, why should I? Furthermore, who was I supposed to witness to at the Christian school? Everyone had already heard about Jesus. We had done more than our share of practice in Bible class: what to say, how to say it, and how to counter any argument that may arise. I was ready to put it into practice.

Besides, I had already been feeling inadequate on account of the Mormons. In my family, the Mormons were the topic of many a heated dinner conversation. Dad had attended Brigham Young University and had studied them up close and personal for the duration of his graduate studies. At church, he had become somewhat of an unofficial spokesperson against what he referred to as "cults" with an expertise in Mormonology. For our family vacation one summer, he even drove us off the beaten path to western New York to see the Hill of Cumorah, the site where the Mormons believe the angel Moroni visited Joseph Smith and gave him the Golden Plates. He was adamantly opposed to their theology, of course. Even so, he did have an admiration for their dedication and frequently cited their mandatory two-year mission as something we could learn from.

As a teenager who wanted nothing more than to be a "radical" Christian, I felt ashamed in comparison. I needed to do more than "talk the talk"—I needed to "walk the walk." People's souls were at stake. It was time to do my part and step up to the call. The Rapture was on its way, and I had no business wasting my time around other Christians.

I chose the school I should have attended for my neighborhood were it not for the Christian school. But even though it was a school with kids mostly from mid- to upper-income families, it was not without its own seedy underbelly. The school came complete with a smoking section in the courtyard, foul-mouthed teachers and condom distribution in the nurse's office.

It was perfect.

Spying my opportunity to get in quick with the heathens, I promptly enrolled in a class called "Music, Theater, Dance," in which I learned all sorts of racy skills, including how to do a shuffle-ball-step and the five positions in ballet. When I found myself enjoying what I was doing a little too much, I reminded myself that I was there for a purpose. Certain sacrifices had to be made for the good of the cause and if that meant I had to learn to step in time, so be it. And when the predicted date of the Rapture came and went without incident, I saw it as an even bigger opportunity to make an impact. Now I had the whole year to bring public school kids to Jesus. King Richard had nothing on me that year.

It was in "Music, Theater, Dance" class that I met Mary. Mary lived down the street from me; was intelligent, funny, and most importantly, an agnostic.

"Sure, God might exist," she told me early into our friendship after I shoved the subject in her lap like a brightly wrapped present. "But She might not, too. How the hell should I know?"

Guide to Churchese

Godliness – 1. The thoughtful conformity to how one perceives God would live, were He indeed just a slob like one of us. 2. Often confused with pretending one is actually God in matters of judgment, piety, and denial of human desires.

Agnostic Mary let her red curly hair run free down her back, had playful eyes the color of glacier water and was unapologetically profane. She had a boyfriend who was a few years older than she was and loved to tell me about what they did together. Entire one-sided conversations about the various sexual positions and the woes of birth control occurred between us during scat lessons and demi-pliés. Watching her was like watching a circus train filled with sin, with brightly colored props and body parts spilled all along the tracks. I couldn't look away. We would move on together from that class to English, in which we spent whole sessions drawing caricatures of our teacher.

I was appalled and fascinated all at once. I think she was equally fascinated by me as I had little to no clue what she was talking about half the time. But even though I was shocked by her, I adored her. She had a witty intelligence and she was kind...and practical in her kindness. I once saw her sneak off down the street under pretense of needing to get a better look at something and handing off a pastry she had just bought to a homeless person we had passed half a block back. When she returned she didn't even say anything about it. She just continued along with some filthy story she was telling before the interruption.

I had seen the same homeless person she had, but my reaction had been to grip my purse tighter and keep my eyes facing front. A saint she was not, but she had a heart for others that I envied. At one point in our friendship, I would walk in on a conversation she and Scott were having. In the background, Pink Floyd sang "On the Turning Away" and Mary was talking about her dream to try to get a ski resort to donate a free skiing day, complete with transportation, food and gear, for the homeless. The way she spoke of it, it was clear she had given it a lot of thought.

It was weird. She acted like a Christian, only not. Let me restate that. She treated other people like Jesus would have done, only she didn't act godly. She did not *act like a Christian*. She took the Lord's name in vain. She didn't clean up her mouth just because she was around me, despite the fact that I listened to CCM—*Christian Contemporary Music*— instead of Nine Inch Nails or Depeche Mode and made a point to substitute "darn" for "damn."

She had sex. *Real* sex.

She confused me.

I took her on as my project. I wanted to lead her to the Lord. I was sure that it was for her that I had been led to that school. For whatever reason, she didn't mind hanging out with me and even invited me over to her house—an event that caused quite a stir in my household as her father was a professed atheist and her mother was a non-practicing Catholic, a revelation that required the use of smelling salts on my parents. When they came to, I explained that I felt God had led me to her and not to worry. I wouldn't allow our friendship to interfere with my own spirituality and turn me into a backslidden heathen.

I knew that if I wanted to save her, I couldn't mess around. Her father didn't scare me. Except maybe a little. On account of the fact that he was godless. There were probably demons hanging thickly around him all the time. I supposed his eyes even glowed red in the dark. But I would not have to be alone in the room with him at any point, I was fairly certain. I was there to see his daughter, after all, not him. And while she had not expressly said anything about giving her heart to Jesus, I just knew that she was going to crack any day. Finally, Mom and Dad reluctantly conceded, made a prayer of protection over me, and let me go.

In English class, I ventured to talk to her about spiritual things. I was so worried about her. By now she was my friend. *Truly* my friend. I cared about her. Maybe we could start a conversation and it could go from there and by the final bell she would be ready. We could sit in her room later and say a prayer together and that would be it. She would be saved. We could be BFFs, literally *forever*. She just seemed so distracted lately, and the truth was, I felt like I had no idea if I was making any impact or not. I feared that if she didn't give her heart to the Lord soon, my parents were going to force our friendship to come to an end. They were losing patience with me and the time I was spending on "that girl."

But "that girl" had become special to me.

Even so, I still had faith that it would happen. I had been praying hard. More than our friendship, I knew that it was her soul that was at stake, and I prayed like I had never prayed before.

I was just getting ready to make a segue comment about how the book we were reading for class reminded me of symbolism in the Bible, when she said it.

"I'm late," she whispered, peeking up over her book, her pale blue eyes narrowed at me.

I glanced up at the wall clock.

"We got a few more minutes," I assured her, thinking that she was referring to a quiz we were going to be taking at the end of class. It wasn't like her to be behind in her reading. I shook my head, thinking about how distracted she had been that day. In "Music, Theater, Dance" class, she had barely even tried when it was time to practice our glitter fingers. *Late*, I thought with a grimace. What I wanted to say was that we were running out of time to save her soul and that she should put a little more thought and effort toward being on time for that.

"No, I mean I'm *laaaate*."

I sat there blinking at her, clueless as Normandy on June 5th, 1944.

"Are you serious?" she hissed across the aisle, shocked that I was so dimwitted. "Late? As in my period?"

"Oh," I answered quickly, realizing how stupid I had been. I admit, I have always been a bit slow in matters regarding a woman's *special time*. My sweet mother—bless her—had made an attempt once at explaining things to me. Her intro was something along the lines of, "Perhaps you have noticed a little blue box on the back of my toilet? Would you like to talk about what that's for?" But as I was already 12 at the time, I had already been filled in at least at some level in Health class. How could anyone forget the fascinating little film featuring a silhouette of the male and female forms with hair *actually growing* to fill in the underarms and pubic regions? And when a subject is taboo for so long—even after you know what's up—it is positively mortifying to speak of it with your mother. It was at this point that I informed her I already knew all about that, thus ending our only discussion in recorded history on the topic.

"Wait. Did you say you're late?"

She nodded.

"Because...oh. OH." Suddenly it hit me. How was this even possible? She was only 15.

"Oh my God," said Mary.

"Mary!" She did *not* just take the Lord's name in vain. She knew how I felt about that!

"Sorry, I'm just —" She covered her forehead. "Never mind."

Throughout the rest of the day I watched for an opportunity to talk more to Mary. She was going to be a mother. I reeled at the thought. How does that even work at 15? Would she keep going to school and have her non-practicing Catholic mother watch the child? Would her devil father take an active role in his grandchild's life? Would he paint upside down crosses in the nursery when no one was looking? Draw pentagrams under the crib? My mind shut down at that point. Things were spiraling out of control fast. I had to do something.

Every time I saw her, though, she seemed to barely even notice I was there. It was almost as if she was avoiding me, although I couldn't imagine why. It was not until we were walking toward the bus that I finally cornered her.

"So, what are you doing this weekend?" I asked nonchalantly, thinking that when she asked me what I was doing back I could casually mention that I was going to church and she could come with me. You know, if she wanted to. She was going to need a support system, after all. I matched her step for step on our way behind the school to where the buses waited for us.

"I don't know. I think I'm going to be out sick for a couple of days. I think my mom is going to take me to the clinic tomorrow. I don't know if I'll be back before the weekend or not."

I wrinkled up my brow at her. All around us, other students laughed and shouted, their voices echoing hollow off the brick buildings.

"What's wrong? You feeling OK?" I asked, thrown off guard for a minute.

"Nothing. I'm fine," she said, smiling with closed lips and patting me on the shoulder. "Why? What are you doing this weekend?"

I blinked at her as it sank in. The clinic? There was an unmistakable sadness in her eyes.

"Are you sure? I mean, you don't have to do that...." I trailed off, suddenly unsure of myself. I was in unfamiliar territory. By the look on her face I could see that she was, too.

"Not even my choice. My parents' decision."

I opened my mouth—ready to object, argue, tell her she just needed to trust Jesus—but no words came out. Instead, it suddenly hit me—the gravity of it all. I had been so wrapped up in wanting to convert her, to save her soul, that I had missed the pain she was in. And now, she was telling me that she was about to have an abortion and that there was nothing she—or I, for that matter—could do to stop it.

An abortion. Ending a human life before it had the chance to really even begin. I knew how I felt about that. It was wrong. Had someone asked me before I had met Mary, I would have flushed five shades of self-righteous and declared that she was a sinner of criminal proportions. Certainly my church would not have stood for it. And if my parents had known what was going on in that moment, they would have insisted I never speak with her again—not until she "cleaned up," found Jesus, and was at least as pious as the rest of us.

"I'm 15," she said. There was fear in her eyes. "I messed up. I don't want to mess up somebody else's life, too. Not because of my stupid mistake."

I saw it then. More than ever before, she just needed a friend. Somebody to lean on. Forget the idea of Hell in the shadowy Great Someday. She was going through hell right then, and I was missing it.

An Exorcise in Faith

If you "grew up Evangelical" like I did, then you fIt into one of three categories: either you left, you stayed, or you're banging your head repeatedly somewhere in the middle.

Depending on where you fit in relation to these three categories, you may have a different comfort level when talking about your past church days.

For example, maybe you were the kid who saw it as your mission to convert the Goth Girl at your high school. She may have dressed in all black, recited lyrics from The Cure from the corner of the lunchroom and threatened you with a broken vodka bottle every time you came near her, but she needed Jesus, too. Maybe you single-handedly coordinated this introduction. Gathered some friends while she was smoking in the bathroom and circled her stall. Joined hands and told her Jesus loves her before launching into "Amazing Grace." Maybe she emerged from that smoky stall with wet, mascara-smeared eyes and repented...and maybe she didn't.

If you are someone with this nugget in your past and your current status with the Evangelical church is "clean break," you are likely experiencing this memory with a cold sweat.

If you currently count yourself amongst the card-carrying flock, however, you may have fond memories of that moment. It is possible that you remember that event with a twinge of pride. But if you are anything like I was for many years, somewhere indefinably in-between, this experience will only serve to fill you with confusion.

On the one hand, joining together for the forces of good against what you believed to be the forces of evil was a brave action to administer. You were doing what you believed to be the work of God. Furthermore, you weren't hurting anyone. You simply wanted Goth Girl to know that she didn't have to be so sad and constantly compelled to light the school on fire. Jesus loved her—and YOU loved her enough to let her know that.

Guide to Churchese

Demon Possession — 1. What happens when a demon takes over a body for the purposes of its own ill intent. May include but is not limited to: blasphemy, taunting messages, and bizarre gymnastics.

On the other hand, Goth Girl wasn't actually hurting anyone. What she was experiencing was an important part of her own development and journey. It is even possible that a lot of the anger she was expressing was due to a lack of understanding from others about her need to express her individuality. What if whenever she called the 2nd period English teacher a "spectacularly hopeless bitchtard," what she was really saying was, "I am a creative and intelligent human being and this class caters too much toward the average student. Please, challenge me with Kafka, Joyce and Faulkner so that I may fly on the wings of the great writers of the past to someday become a Nobel Laureate."?

Perhaps when you gang-prayed her in the bathroom, she only came out with a contrite heart because she had been fighting against conformity for so long that she finally gave

in. Maybe it stuck, maybe it didn't. The bigger issue is that
her conversion may very well have been coerced at a time when
she was vulnerable and weak, and had nothing to do with an
independent decision on her part to jump rails on her own
spiritual path. It was a case of peer pressure. For better or for
worse, this thought may be somewhat humbling.

My experience was similar, and yet different. The Goth
Girl didn't go to my school; she went to my church. Actually,
she only sometimes went to my church, presumably because
she was too busy on Sunday mornings sleeping off an absinthe
binge or possibly standing on a street corner somewhere
hurling rocks at passing vehicles. But while she did not
regularly end up sulking in a pew, she did end up at church
camp one year. Whether she arrived there voluntarily or not
is a bit of a debate—regardless, with the constant activities
and sheer mass of adult counselors, she had nowhere to run
to baby, nowhere to hide. And like Goth Girl of the public
school above, my story begins in the bathroom, too.

*

I leaned one hip against a sink and glanced tentatively at
the stall door to my right, cringing as I suppressed a wave of
nausea and trying to think of other things to distract myself.
The way the sun looked as it rose over the ponderosas that
morning. The way the fluorescent lights made my acne stand
out in the mirrors.

It was no use. There is simply no pleasant way to listen to
somebody puking in a public restroom.

Personally, I am not one overly prone to throwing up.
Once, when I got some pieces of bailing wire caught in my
tonsils due to a bizarre Youth Group Harvest Fest hay ride

incident, my mom made me swallow a tablespoon or two full of Ipecac in order to attempt to force it out. She was certain that a piece of hay had simply lodged itself in my throat and needed to be encouraged upwards. She made me take the vile elixir because after an hour of tears and unsuccessful attempts at sticking my finger down my throat and forceful half-grunts which made me sound like a constipated Neanderthal, I could not self-induce vomiting.

All this is to say that vomiting was a relatively new sensation to me at the time, having had perhaps only one or two incidences prior, somewhere in my early, hazy youth. And while puking up the contents of my stomach did not turn out to be a successful method of bailing line extraction (I would need minor surgery for that), I did learn something about myself: I had a serious handicap. Certainly, when I actually needed the skill, I was not able to produce, leaving me somewhat defunct in the area. Which is why I have a kind of weird respect for bulimics. And Tudors. And anybody who can produce vomit on demand, actually.

So when I stood, listening, grimacing and holding down my own impotent gag reflex as Megan retched behind the closed stall door, I have to admit that I was not only disgusted beyond belief, but I was also impressed as hell. When she finally emerged after several minutes of agonized retching, she leaned against the door, exhausted.

"I was throwing up demons," she informed me with hollow eyes. "I thought I was done, but they just kept coming."

I glanced behind her at the shimmering fresh bowl, and wondered if they were down in the camp's septic system.

Earlier that afternoon, we had been enjoying turkey sandwiches in the cafeteria. We never had our expectations set very high for the food at church camp. We were under no illusions that Rachael Ray was hard at work behind the closed doors to the kitchen. As such, we had made the best we could of what we were given. Now, however, I was wishing that I had passed on lunch.

I had sat next to Megan in the lunchroom because there was something about her that intrigued me. She was part of the classification of teenager we called "New Wave," which would later be called "Goth" and sometimes "Emo" in its millennial reiterations. She wore all black clothing, dark eye makeup and lipstick, and had by her own admission done a fair amount of experimentation in the arena of hallucinogens—information that might have proved useful had I been aware of what that really meant during the time I was sharing a cabin with her.

In retrospect, I am not entirely certain what would have inspired me to keep such company back then in my "über-Christian" state, but I believe I was trying to convert her. It was no secret that she was a troubled youth, if ever there was one. And still, she had a sweet personality. She was always friendly to Scott and me. When she set down her half-eaten sandwich and whispered to me that she was having flashbacks, I was on it. I asked her if she wanted to go lie down. She murmured something about spiders crawling on her hands and nodded emphatically. Seeing my chance to be a good friend, I let her hold onto my arm as we walked back alone through the woods to our cabin, all the while becoming more and more freaked out as she narrated what she was seeing around her. That tree was a dog a second ago. There was an old man peeking at us from behind that tree. And behind the next, another man stood with an axe.

By the time we got to the empty cabin, I was ready. I knew about this sort of thing. I had heard about a girl who had been through an exorcism. She, sadly, had been inhabited by a

"Laughing Demon" right in the middle of Youth Group—and there was nothing funny about it.

"Megan, I think we should pray," I told her, leaning up against a ladder to a top bunk. She stood facing me from a couple of feet away, blinking. Since she didn't argue, I started right in. I had just gotten to the part where I asked God in Jesus' name to protect Megan, when I felt like I was being watched. I looked up.

"Stop praying," the voice told me.

It was Megan's voice, only not. Lower. Louder. Likewise, her face was her own, only not. Something weird about her eyes. Bigger, more piercing. They were staring hatred clean through me. In truth, they almost looked...reptilian. I stammered a little. I had not exactly expected this. Or maybe I had. At any rate, I attempted to rise to the occasion with Me vs. The Demon, round one.

"In Jesus' name, leave Megan alone," I told it.

She closed her eyes. Whimpered a little. I began to pray harder.

"Don't stop praying," she whimpered at me. "It hurts, but don't stop."

"You have no business here," I told the demon. "I order you back to Hell where you belong."

"Shut up," it told me firmly, cold eyes glaring at me once again. Another shock went through my body as I stared back at her.

"In Jesus' name come out of her and leave her alone," I repeated, to which it replied by shaking Megan's body violently before throwing her like a ragdoll onto one of the lower beds, where she proceeded to pass out.

I stood there, staring at her, unsure of what to do next. Had the demon left? Does one touch a person when they are passed out due to demon infestation? Is it contagious? I was not given the chance to find out. That was when she jumped up and ran to the bathroom, where she began puking up demons along with her turkey sandwich.

I stood there at the stall door contemplating whether what I had just witnessed was real. Since then, I have watched *The Exorcism of Emily Rose*, and I can honestly say that it was nothing like that. There were no simultaneous voices jeering at me in German, Latin, Hebrew and Aramaic. The only thing I heard was in plain English ordering me to stop praying. There were no amazing feats of contortion. Megan ran on her own two feet in a balanced manner without the bizarre compulsion to defy the bounds of human joints or the laws of gravity. I did not witness a Cirque de Soleil demon. But I must also say that at the time, it felt just as real as if I had.

And, I had no idea whether I had just won or lost. Unlike the Catholics, there are not exactly any commonly known exorcism rites in the Evangelical church. It's more or less a matter of ordering a demon out of somebody in Jesus' name and sitting back and letting the unseen powers battle it out amongst themselves. The guys in white versus the guys in red. And now, I knew I had to take the responsibility to lead her to Christ—so the demon didn't come back with friends (or "Legion", as the Bible puts it). But as it was, I had no assurance that what I had done was adequate.

I decided that there was only one thing left to do. Take her to King Richard for Round 2. He would know what to do. His primary occupation outside of the church was dealing with the heathens around town; he would surely recognize what was going on. I was just sure he had seen more than his fair share of demon-infested people during his bar ministry.

When she was done hacking up demons, we made our way gingerly back toward the cabin with her holding on to my arm for support. Fortunately, people were coming back from lunch and I spotted Richard's blond strands bouncing in the wind like glory. Clearly, God had positioned him right where he needed to be. I called out to him. He turned almost as if he had been expecting me. I felt a sense of relief wash over me. Everything was going to be OK.

But everything was not going to be OK. That was when it all fell apart. As soon as Megan understood that Richard had been summoned, she let go of me faster than I could process and took off. I tried chasing her for several steps, but she was clearly faster than I ever would be with a pair of high tech track shoes and professional training. Whatever demons were left in her had specializations in long-distance running.

I fell back, feeling defeated and bewildered.

*

Later that week when I got home, I tried to explain to my mother what had happened. My mother—who managed to shame me with the level of how impressed she was that Megan could vomit on demand if the whole thing had been a hoax— simply shook her head, commenting that the whole thing sounded "bizarre." My father, on the other hand, seemed ignited by my story, leading me to a bookshelf he used for his more "interesting" collection of books. Seeming to think that I had suddenly come of age through the experience, he stacked several books on the floor marked with various pentagrams and large red lettering describing how the Church of Satan was alive and well and threatening Christ's church through rock music and subliminal advertising.

"I think you'll find these interesting," he told me. Together, we leafed through the pages and talked about what might be happening on the other side of the veil. It was one of our favorite topics, with me plying him with questions and him answering with what the scriptures had to say on various topics. And while he was never quick to say "this is how it is," we would spend hours talking together about "how it might be," with each of us trying to one-up the other on what we knew about what the Bible had to say on the topic, and in what version. It was fun. Like a game. He opened my mind to possibilities, while at the same time challenging me to look closely at the options. More than anyone, my father taught me to question.

"There are a lot of things we don't understand, honey," he would say whenever we would come to a stalemate on a topic. "Maybe someday we will, but for now they will just have to remain a mystery." Then he would put an arm around my shoulders and pull me in close. "Just remember, we're on this path together. You, me, all of the people you come in contact with every day. As nice as it would be, it's not up to us to have every little thing figured out. It's our job to love each other."

Stairway to Cheez Whiz

Despite my parents' best efforts, I think it's fair to say that I failed them in the music department. The thing is, I love rock 'n roll. Love hip-hop. Love the Beatles clear on through to the Beastie Boys.

To my family, this is a whole world of wrongs. I was not only NOT allowed to listen to secular radio when I was a kid, but I was also subjected to the cultural alternative at least daily. My mother, being a professional harpist, took the lead on this, lulling us to sleep with the classics every night. When I wasn't busy doing my homework, I was polishing my shoes so that I could make an appearance at one of the weekly recitals or symphonies being put on either by the city or one of the local universities.

And then there were the music lessons. Oh yes, I play. As a matter of fact I have at one time or another taken lessons for the piano, the violin, the flute, the guitar, the harmonica, the autoharp, the organ, voice, the recorder, and—oh yes—the harp.

After the failed Rapture and a year at the public school, I decided to head back over to the Christian school. Life at the public school was hard, I'll admit. Ideas there were challenging. People did not really understand where I was coming from. Going back to the Christian school was just easier. Even so, the public school had changed me. In some ways I was even more sure of my faith, and in other ways, I was less sure about what I was supposed to be doing. Part of that mini-rebellion was in the music I listened to. Now, I was sneaking the radio and even MTV. It was the era of Vanilla Ice and Bel Biv Devoe, so you know what I'm talking about when I say that the whole world had gone mad. Lucifer, the Lord of Music and the Dance, had dug his long, black nails in deep to the music industry and was holding on for dear life.

When experts in the church said there were Satanic messages which were embedded backwards in rock n' roll music, it seemed all the more credible to me. With the failed Rapture behind us, I was already doing something I wasn't supposed to be by listening to that smut on the sly. The demons were all but slapping high fives over me.

Apparently I was not the only one. Rumor had it that entire groups of boys and girls from the Christian Academy were listening to the stuff. At home, in cars...it was getting out of control. And if anyone needed proof, all one had to do was say "Stop. Hammertime!" in the hallway in between classes and watch the mayhem that would ensue.

Once the alarm had been rung that the Christian Academy's boys and girls were on the fast-track to becoming Hell's hand servants, it was time to bring in the big guns. Clearly, the youth did not understand what it was messing with. We did not appreciate that we were dealing with powers and principalities unseen. On Monday, all of that would change.

Both to our joy and apprehension, we arrived at school to find that we were on chapel schedule that day—despite the fact it was not a normal day for chapel. But what they had to tell us could not wait.

We filed in reverently to the chapel auditorium. The anticipation was so thick that nobody was really talking to anybody else. I sat near the front wedged in between one of the boys from the varsity basketball team and a woman teacher who had the annoying habit of sniffling every ten seconds. To make matters worse, one of them smelled like tuna fish.

But I would not dwell on this for long. Just as I feared I was about to faint from nausea, the lights were dimmed and a large movie screen at the front demanded our undivided attention. Rock music blared. Colored lights and flashy lightning-bolt-styled graphics assaulted our retinas. Some of the boys—apparently accustomed to worshipping the Dark Lord through music—began pulsing their heads to the rhythm. And then all faded to black.

Guide to Churchese

Backmasking – The deliberate placement of messages on musical tracks which sound like gobbledeegook played forwards, and a clear message played backwards. Usually the backwards message is so sneaky that it also rarely sounds like anything—which is why a person with an intense, conspiratorial voice is required to translate for you before any understanding may be reached that you are receiving a Satanic message.

Over the course of the next hour, my eyes and ears were opened. What I hadn't known until that moment was that I had been allowing myself to be controlled. Since the time I had heard my very first rock n' roll song, I had been listening to secret messages from Satan *without even knowing it.*

In numb shock I listened as Led Zeppelin sang an anthem to the Dark Lord when the words "a bustle in your hedgerow" were played backwards in "Stairway to Heaven" producing "Here's to my sweet Satan." At the time, I had never heard of "Stairway to Heaven," being more of a Madonna, Prince and Michael Jackson girl, myself. Never mind the fact that I had never heard any of these artists above a whisper from my clock radio when I knew my parents were on the other side of the house. But what did that matter? If Satan had polluted one song, what was stopping him from polluting them all?

I listened in rapt awe as the evidence unfolded. Queen told us backwards in "Another One Bites the Dust" that "it's fun to smoke marijuana." And then Jefferson Starship, telling us about the "son of Satan" in "A Child is Coming" and the Electric Light Orchestra telling us backwards that "He is the nasty one/ Christ, you're infernal/It is said we're dead men/ Everyone who has the Mark will live."

We learned that it was not our fault—that we could not consciously detect that there was a subliminal message hidden in the forward running text of a song. But it was still there, just waiting for our extraordinary brains to interpret and internalize it—even without our permission.

Some messages were deliberate and clear when played backwards, like the backmasked message from Electric Light Orchestra that "Music is reversible, but time—Turn back! Turn back!" Others were less clear. "It's fun to smoke marijuana," for example, sounded a lot more like "Sfun scout mare wanna," if it weren't for the handy text samples printed concurrently with the backwards message. And I could really only make out a word that sounded like "Satan" in the several phrases that were really secret messages to win us to the Evil One. But that just proved how secret the messages were.

That night, my dreams were riddled with imagery. To this day, I still remember clips. There was a man who looked like a goat with hooves for feet, and a man with long, curly ladies hair and a black tongue which stuck out of his mouth. He was trying to eat me. Bridget from the slumber party was there, too. She wore dark rouge like a mistress of the night and kept trying to tickle me. We were in her room alone with a hot pink canopy over her bed and the stars that looked like pentagrams.

When I woke up the next day, my heart was beating fast as if I had run a marathon. Clearly, something had been communicating with me secretly over the years, causing me to have dreams like that. I went straight to my tape collection and dumped it out on the bed in search of anything suspicious. I spied a couple of Amy Grants and a Michael W. Smith in the mix and set them protectively to one side. Surely, they weren't to blame for anything. A Mozart collection I had in my possession lay loose on the bed. Mozart was no born-again Christian, I was pretty sure—but backward messages? My eyes settled on "The Magic Flute." The Greek god Pan played the flute. I flung it from my sight.

Then came my Bobby McFerrin. That was just what the Devil wanted us to do—to not worry and be happy. I pitched it into the trash before I had time to allow Satan's messengers to instruct me otherwise. I took a deep breath and knelt down by the side of the bed and prayed as hard as I could, begging for forgiveness and cleansing from any evil-doing that I hadn't known that I had done. There. It was over. I had a clean slate.

But it wasn't over.

That weekend I arrived at Sunday school to discover that we had a special speaker. I am not sure how Pastor Mark had caught wind of the recent spate of rock n' roll music at the Christian Academy. It might have been Richard who was responsible for our speaker that day. Like the leadership at my school, he was also all fired up on the issue of backmasking and Satanic influence. Then again, he was always fired up about backmasking and Satanic influence. It is entirely possible that this was just a coincidence.

Whispers and murmurs reverberated in the Lion's Den. What was going to be revealed to us? Was he going to show the same video I had seen at school? I was excited at the thought, as I had hoped Scott could see it. It was just so *effective*. Just that Friday, I had heard in the quiet conversations before and after classes that I had not been alone in my tape disposal efforts. A bunch of the guys in the senior class had gathered all of their tapes together, too, taking turns running over them with a car. I heard that some of the boys even reported screams coming from the tapes as they were crushed beneath the wheels. The car belonged to one of the more popular boys in our class, which served to make the event all the more meaningful. If he had gotten rid of his filthy, Satanic tapes—reportedly a long list, including, but not limited to: Styx, Prince, The Eagles, Dead or Alive, and Chicago—then what was stopping anybody else?

Finally, after Mark and Richard encouraged everyone to find a seat and settle down, a woman we had never seen before approached the front. She had thick salt and pepper hair and wore a purple skirt and blouse ensemble. I reached out and took Scott's hand.

"Hi. My name is Annamaria and I love the Lord. But that wasn't always the case," she told us, reading from her notes. "Eight years ago, I was a member of The Church of Satan."

A gasp rippled through the Youth Group. I had to remind myself to breathe as she told us her story.

It started innocently enough, she told us. She had gone to a friend's house to make chocolate chip cookies and to paint each other's nails. When one of the girls had pulled out a Ouija Board, she had laughed.

My heart started beating in my throat. It was like what had happened to me.

"Put away your silly game," Annamaria told her friend.

But her friend wouldn't listen. If only she had listened. Instead, she watched as her friend began asking it questions, and then receiving answers. She thought it was a trick at first, until her friend convinced her to try it so that she could see first-hand.

"OK, if you're so smart, Mr. Spirit, then what's my favorite song?" she asked, thinking this would surely stump it.

"R-A-D-I-O," it spelled. She scoffed, thinking that "Radio" was hardly a name for a song.

"It's telling you to turn on the radio," her friend informed her. Annamaria rolled her eyes and went over to the radio next to her friend's bed. She turned it on. The song playing was "Devil Went Down to Georgia." It was her favorite song.

She was hooked after that. Whoever or whatever was communicating with Annamaria knew her well. It began to protect her. Once when she and her friends were using the board to communicate with the Spirit, who now went by the name of "Judas," it told her to go to the window. They did—just as a knocking began at a different window. They ran to check it out and the knocking took up on the other side of the house. They began to cry, chasing it back and forth as it knocked. They went back to the board and begged it to stop.

"I will protect you," Judas told her. And sure enough, it stopped.

Later that very night after she left her friend's house, a dog followed her home. The dog stayed with her at a distance the entire time. And no harm came to her. It wasn't long after that when she found a group of people in the Church of Satan and she joined. It was a short leap from there to reading unholy scriptures backwards and sacrificing chickens.

We listened with our hearts in our throats as Annamaria told us story after story. We the members of the Lion's Den already knew that Satan and his demons were real, but we had never actually known somebody who claimed to converse with them. She warned us to stay away—that once you were sucked in, it was extremely difficult to get out.

That kind of presentation makes an impression on a teenager. From that point on, I was careful to only listen to Christian music. No more sneaking the bad stuff in. I didn't dare! And besides, CCM was almost as good as the secular rock. It had a beat and cool lyrics. If you weren't listening very carefully, you might even be fooled into thinking that Amy Grant or Michael W. Smith were singing to their boyfriend or girlfriend instead of God, which was kind of awesome because I could sing the lyrics to God like a love song to Him. Like He was my boyfriend. It was totally cool. And the music was cool. Not necessarily original or innovative in any way, but the perfect substitute. Well, maybe not the *perfect* substitute, but it served its purpose of allowing us teenagers to have our fun music without the threat of Satan.

As for the rock n' roll that almost destroyed my soul, I was done with it. Well, mostly done with it. I did occasionally continue to listen to the Oldie's station on account of the fact that the lyrics were generally cleaner. It didn't exactly occur to me to question whether there was another way to look at the evidence we were presented. I mean, there had been lights and cool graphics and scary voices and wicked looking men with ladies hair and a real live woman who had been through it. It didn't occur to me to ask the important questions. Questions like: "If we played any sample of singing backwards, would we find something that kinda sorta sound like something kinda sorta Satanic, too?" or "If you closed your eyes during the supposed subliminal message and didn't read the text concurrently, would it resemble at all what we were being told it resembled? Did anybody else think that the written text translations of what we were hearing were stretching it just a wee bit?"

I was just 15. I didn't think much about applying the scientific method yet.

I was just 15. I didn't think to question whether anybody had checked Annamaria's references and ruled out any possible mental disorders.

I was just a teenager. I didn't know yet that if you play Amy Grant backwards, you can find creepy phrases there, too. Or if you play Weird Al Yankovic's "Nature Trail to Hell" backwards, you can find "Satan eats Cheez Whiz."

Like I said, I was just 15. And I bought it all.

But more importantly, I learned a behavioral pattern that would carry through to adulthood and pervade my entire worldview: I learned how to substitute.

If something was sinful that I did not want to live without, I found something that placated the desire without having to deal with the guilty feelings. In other words, I learned the loopholes. I exchanged rock n' roll for CCM. I switched foul language like "damn" to "darn." Instead of taking the Lord's name in vain, I said, "My word." I watched Christian movies or read books as much as possible instead of their secular counterparts that might have had strong language or any sexuality. Instead of going to haunted houses at Halloween I went to Fall Fest. Instead of going to dances with friends from the public school, I went to Youth Group all nighters.

Once you start learning how to avoid the bad things without having to suffer, it is easy to keep going. It's just a frame of mind, really. When my mom told me she thought chocolate was causing my face to break out into the worst acne case known to humankind, I switched from Snickers to Paydays. When we thought butter was the worst thing imaginable, we switched to margarine. When bacon was considered to be an even worse atrocity, we switched to Sizzlean.

And later—much later—instead of asking genuine questions and seeking genuine answers, I accepted the standardized clichés that seemed to summarize everything so neatly without actually saying anything. "Ask and ye shall receive...but sometimes God says *no*." "It's just one of those mysteries." "God will never give you more than you can bear." I exchanged actually helping people in need like I was supposed to be doing for burying my nose in my church community and becoming absorbed in the pattern of worship—fellowship—worship—fellowship.

In short, I exchanged a genuine life of *seeking through experience* for one that was defined for me in order to keep me from feeling anything that might make me real.

I Can't Believe It's Not Prom

Evangelicals who grew up in the mid-to-late 80s and beyond share a special bond. This is largely due to a recognizable movement to make the church more "relatable" to Americans, who had been abandoning churches at a steady rate since the late 1950s. During this era we saw a sharp rise in community outreach programs, Christian bookstores and even cushier pews. Most importantly, we saw a push for cooler, hipper youth programs. Think church is boring? Think again. We're *radical*. And we're just like you.

Thus, CCM was on the rise with bands like Stryper and Petra filling city arenas. Christian bookstores began to crop up all over the country and were filled with Christian versions of romance and suspense novels. Camps for youth became more interactive with bigger and better activities—activities like rappelling, hair-raising ropes courses, dune buggies and even parasailing. Christian theme parks like Heritage USA and The Holy Land Experience were rising (and falling). Make no mistake: we had a lot of fun. Anything you wanted, we could offer a Christian substitute. This was important so that we could bring new people into the fold. Jesus himself had given us that mission in the Bible.

*

As our senior year came to a close, our thoughts were basically the same as every other teenager's this side of the waters: time for prom. Well, not exactly prom. Prom at the public school, we were well aware, would have meant a large, marginally supervised dance in the school gymnasium where kids proceed to get stealthily drunk by spiked punch and end up having a giant orgy on the gym floor.

For the conservative Evangelical, the ability to resist attending a prom is the culmination of years of teaching and denial. A final exam, if you will. Of course, most kids in the Youth Group still want to attend prom. For those who attend public school, they have already been bombarded with daily announcements over the intercom of the upcoming event and possibly a skit or two put on by the short-skirted cheerleaders in school assembly. But only the weakest members of the Youth Group actually attend their school prom, thus exposing themselves to the rest of the flock as long-toothed pagans wearing a no-longer convincing swatch of lamb pelt across their shoulders.

Thus was born SNAZ at my church.

SNAZ was a grand event. It had all the trimmings of prom, with none of the sin. It was the ultimate substitution event. It was the Sizzlean of the formal event world. It was so good nobody could believe it wasn't butter. Already we had substitution events for Halloween (Fall Fest) as well as our own Valentine's banquet. We didn't have to listen to real rock n' roll. We had Youth Group and weekend activities to keep us so busy we didn't have to think about sex, focusing our love on God instead. But SNAZ trumped all of those.

We, the Youth Group teens, were to get gussied up for the event, bring a date if one could be found, and attend a dinner of grandiose scale—complete with crepe paper and candlelight—and listen to a sermon about how awesome it was that we weren't off breeding under disco light-scattered bleachers like bacteria in a Petri dish. After this impressive evening, we would be treated to an overnighter at the Recreation Center, a Christian "Afterprom", where we would party in style. All. Night. Long.

Scott and I were stoked. Having made the mistake the year before of attending Scott's school prom, I knew all too well what the pressures of such an event were like. Scott was on his student council and was, therefore, responsible for helping to put on the event. What else could we do but go? Walking

Guide to Churchese

Purity — Evangelical believers are admonished to practice activities that are considered "pure" so that they may be considered worthy by Christ. This generally means abstaining from all the big, obvious soul-stainers like murder and lying, but in the Youth Group context involves mostly sexual abstinence, which is generally pledged to God and one's daddy. Does not include abstinence from crockpots full of spicy, processed substances and/or Jello marshmallow salads.

into his school auditorium dressed in a black and white polka dotted formal, I could feel the dark cloud of oppression immediately weighing on my heart. Even so, something about that atmosphere crept quickly under my skin and I admittedly lost myself for a while. A stray stream of light from a large disco ball hanging down from the exposed pipes caught me in the eye and suddenly it was as if everything I had been taught had been flushed down the drain. Before I knew it, I was pulling Scott manically toward the center of the floor so that we could dance to Mr. Roboto with a group of his friends from the council.

Somehow, we managed to escape permanent stigma in the Youth Group from the attendance of that prom—partly because we kept it quiet, and partly because we decided that we had only attended as a mission of sorts to Scott's heathen classmates as demonstrated to us by King Richard and his infamous bar ministry. So when SNAZ appeared on the radar the following year, we were admittedly relieved.

I had the perfect outfit: a royal purple floor length, strapless gown with long gloves dyed to match. Scott would strive to match me with a crisp rented tux complete with long tails, cumber bun and bowtie, also dyed to match by the same purple soup.

Everyone looked fantastic. Girls and boys with dates wore the ubiquitous corsages and boutonnières. A cloud of Polo, Poison, and Giorgio mixed with the subtle infusion of Aqua Net hung in the Lion's Den like a fog. Enough makeup was worn collectively by the females of the species to clean out the entire Cover Girl section at Wal-Mart. Pastor Mark and Deb were dressed tastefully with a black suit and tie for him and a pretty blue dress and pearls for her. When King Richard and Dina arrived in the Lion's Den, we were so impressed that we nearly broke out into full on applause. Dina wore a hot pink drop waist gown made from sateen and crushed velvet. Matching her glitter for shine, Richard appeared in a dark blue tux, albeit an inch or two on the short side, hot pink Converse high tops and a black T-shirt screen-printed with a ruffle and bow tie. His hair had been tussled until it shone. Even his gold cross earring had been buffed until it radiated joy.

Having been washed and polished for the big evening, Gus was ready and waiting for us in the parking lot—each speck of hot pink and sky blue splatter paint visible from beneath its usual crust of ardent ministry. With grace and poise, we carried ourselves and our gym bags for the after-SNAZ activities onto our beloved bus and headed toward the nearby Air Force Base, where a room awaited us.

Inside the dining hall, we were bedazzled by the sheer mass of white lights and hot pink crepe paper that hung over the set tables. From the center of each shone a small white votive, surrounded by black and pink glittery table confetti. We found our names on special cards, which also read: "Blessed are the pure in heart."

We ate our meals in muted gaiety, until a screech from the front turned our attention and signaled the wait staff to collect our plates.

"Sorry about that," Pastor Mark said, just as another screech rent a second hole in the space-time continuum. We laughed dutifully at our esteemed leader's rollicking foibles and turned our chairs so that we could see him better.

"Are you enjoying your meals?" he asked, when the general scuffle of twisting chairs settled down. A few people applauded. And then, after a dramatic pause, he touched the microphone to his lips and said in a low voice something that sounded like, "Pureed."

At first I thought he was going to initiate one of the Youth Group games which involved pureed baby food until he said it again, this time with an inch between his lips and the foam red cover on the microphone.

"Purity," he repeated.

Realizing that this was going to be a talk on the topic of keeping ourselves pure for marriage and not on the viscosity of certain foods, a few of us shifted in our seats. Over the next twenty minutes or so, we listened as Pastor Mark encouraged us to keep ourselves out of the backseats of cars as we strove to keep ourselves pure and holy for Christ. As always, he was dignified and full of grace as he spoke to us. His gentle eyes in combination with fluid hand movements compelled us to trust him. And that's when he said it.

"Some of you have already done an admirable job of staying pure. I'm always so proud when I think of Scott and Erika...."

He went on to compliment our lack of sexual activity to the entire group. Did we deserve that? I'm not so sure we deserved that. After the shift in our private make-out sessions thanks to the Power Team, "pure" was not exactly the word I would have chosen.

It was an awkward moment. There we were, the poster children for purity, and I felt like a bit of a sham. True, we had not had *actual* sex. We had learned our lessons well, after all. Sexuality and spirituality did not and could not mix. But of course, we had learned the loopholes. We had learned the *substitutions*, as it were.

What were we supposed to do? Stand up and correct him? Say something to the effect of, "Actually, Pastor Mark, if you would allow us to clarify to you and the entire Youth Group. While we have yet to have intercourse, I would like to publicly disclose that we have actually done quite a lot in replacement. I mean truly, a lot. As in...everything but. Pretty hot, actually."

No. That was a conversation and a clarification that would just have to be, um, deferred. Or perhaps conveniently omitted. At least until I decided to write a memoir and tell the whole freaking world. After all, what harm could come from not filling our fellow youth groupies in on our sexual status? Or, more importantly, what good could come from it? If everyone knew that we had not been able to completely refrain from what we had been doing, how could that possibly serve as an example to others?

Later that night, after sneaking off to some back stairwell in the rec center after back-to-back bowling for close to three hours, I held up a hand as Scott leaned in to kiss me.

"Stop," I said.

He reared back, clearly confused. He tried again.

"No, seriously."

A heaviness escaped from his soul via his lungs.

"It's what Mark said, isn't it," he stated more than asked.

I nodded.

"I just feel—like such a fraud."

"Erika, you are not a fraud. We have not had sex."

Right. And I did not have a proverbial dress hanging in my closet with a stain providing evidence to the contrary. But as this was the late 80s, and such philosophical advances had not yet been made thanks to the dawn and dusk of the country's next president, I nodded in agreement.

"OK, but I still think that something doesn't feel quite right. I feel like we're not exactly being honest."

He sighed again, somewhere from his gut.

"OK. Do you want me to back off?"

I looked at him with big puppy dog eyes and nodded.

He shook his head.

"All right."

I grinned.

"I love you," I told him.

"I love you, too."

Deftly, I whipped a piece of paper out of my pocket and began to write.

"What are you doing?"

"I'm making a covenant."

"A covenant?"

"Something to keep us on track."

I finished writing and held it out to him. He took it and read aloud.

"I, Scott, promise to be nothing but a gentleman under penalty of lemon juice poured in paper cuts all over my arms and hands." He looked up at me. "Ouch."

I shrugged at him.

"You want me to sign this?"

I handed him my pen.

"Fine," he took the pen. "But just so you know, I will consider this covenant null and void if you ever come to me looking ... for something more."

So resolute was I that I quickly held out my hand.

"Deal."

"Deal," he echoed.

I was so happy that I threw my arms around his neck and gave him a giant hug, pulled him into a nearby janitor's closet...and nullified that contract.

Yeah. SNAZ was just that awesome.

Sharing is Good, Right?

I HAVE HEARD TELL FROM A RELIABLE SOURCE[3] THAT THERE is a time and a place for everything—and it's called college. While in theory this may be true, I think it is glaringly obvious that the purveyor of this dream did not attend an Evangelical university, let alone one located in the giant silver and turquoise-studded buckle of the Great American Bible Belt. Like I did.

Little changes en route from the high school Youth Group to the Christian College. Same rules apply: no swearing, no alcohol, and definitely no sex, although it is only fair to add that these things do actually occur, although not in the open. When one does partake in one of the aforementioned truffles of sin, they must be tasted under the cloak of night and with friends of like mind who would not be tempted to rat you out simply to see you pay a fine or be expelled before you spoiled the rest of the apples. Thus, there exists a deep, dark underground within the confines of the Evangelical University—one so vile and hideous that few know of its existence. In this subversive cavern, one may let the swear words fly freely while simultaneously enjoying all manner of evils, including but not limited to dancing and the drinking of things like wine coolers, which my friend Carissa once pointed out to me are a gateway drug to Zima.

---

3   * Chef, on *South Park*

I was blissfully and naively unaware of such an underground for most of my college years. Like many of my peers, I chose to view college as an extension of my time in the Youth Group, an illusion I managed to perpetuate by the subconscious belief that I was simply away at Youth Camp. There were rules, there were curfews, there was a snack bar...and with mandatory chapel to help keep me on track, I was in no immediate danger of falling into a sandpit lying somewhere in the shadows of our utopian campus.

But why I chose to leave the majestic purple shade of the Rocky Mountains in order to spend "the best years of my life" in a place where the big event of the week was fried livers and gizzards night at a place down the street called Dot's (advertised as "lizards and givers night") continues to elude me. At first, I had been dubious. While it was true that I was an above-average fan of biscuits and gravy and sweet tea, I was not exactly sure that was what I wanted as a college experience. So when both Scott and I received acceptance letters from a college within our denomination, I must admit that I was a bit surprised. He sensed my hesitation.

"Sure, we could choose a more prestigious place and pay through the nose to do it—but the professor I'd be under is at the top of the National Physics Society and he wants to give me free run of the lab. Plus it's small, so we'd get personal attention. And," he hesitated to brush a strand of hair out of my face, "we could make sweet monkey love sooner." OK. That's not what he said. What he really said was, "We could afford to get married sooner." Whatever. Same diff.

With that promise to hang my hat on, I was fully on-board. What could we do? God said it was the place we ought to be, so we loaded up the truck and moved to the city. Oklahoma, that is. Red dirt, country stars. Set a spell. Take yer shoes off. Y'all come back now, y'hear?

*

One of the best things about going to college at a Christian university was that I didn't have to stop going to Youth Group. Not really, anyway. And the best part was that it was not just once a week—it was *three* times a week. I'm talking, of course, about college chapel. True, chapel was an inadequate replacement for the *real* Youth Group we went to in our teenage years. There are no games involving baby food and there is no competition in mind— unless, of course, you count switching off boys and girls singing different verses in a praise chorus ("Now just the ladies!").

Guide to Churchese

Chapel – The place where the student body gathers for the purpose of listening to Christian motivational speakers who may or may not live in a van down by the river. In our case, this large room doubled as a stage for theatrical productions and could seat approximately 1200 people. During chapel, the doors are heavily guarded—not to keep people out, mind you, for all are welcome. You just can't, well, leave.

And while the singing may lack a certain "quality" such as only my former Youth Group leaders, Pastor Mark and King Richard, could bestow upon it, it's not so bad. There might even be a chapel band, which includes a couple of song leaders with guitars and/or tambourines and possibly a drum set.

When I first arrived at college, I was stoked to learn that with the fast approach of autumn, revival was on its way. A giant poster in the lobby of our dorm advertised the upcoming event.

"REVIVAL!" The words hovered in bold, all-caps directly above the perfectly combed hair of a man who, for whatever reason, appeared to be tasting his glasses. While his face was somewhat boyish, anyone could see that he was wise in preacher years. At the bottom of the poster, he was described as the possessor of gifts to inspire us to renew our commitments to the Lord. According to the poster, Revivalist John Calvin Smart had led thousands to the Lord—including "several hundred in South America, Africa and Canada"—and specialized in talking to young people about relationships and the sanctity of marriage. For anyone who took the time to stop and read between the lines, it was clear that Pastor Smart was going to talk to us about sex.

If there is one thing that an Evangelical teenager loves to talk about, it's sex. We just talk and talk and talk. And we love it. Second to Jesus, there is no more fully covered topic within the Youth Group:

- How to avoid it
- How much more fulfilling our lives will be for not having it
- How many of our godless peers are having it
- How much after all that talk we still can't wait to have it

But anyone could see by the solemn look in Pastor Smart's eyes and the perfection of grooming on top of his solid head, he meant business. He was not messing around—and neither, said his hair, should we.

A week went by and finally the day came when we would see Pastor Smart live and in the unadulterated flesh. When my American Lit class was over that morning, I practically flew to the chapel auditorium. I could hardly wait—and from the buzz of my fellow classmates filing into the auditorium on the long-awaited day, neither could anybody else.

From outside the building, the jubilant tinkling of an old-timey piano compelled us forward. Squinting over the heads in the line in front of me, I could see that Pastor Smart's whole family was up there on that stage. His wife was the one responsible for the holy rollin' stylings on the piano, of course. To her right, their three children jammed beside her. Farthest from her was a boy of about 14 who played a mean saxophone. Periodically, he would let it hang on the strap around his neck while he clapped his hands out in front of his chest, inciting the congregation to various whoops and hollers. Next in line was a girl who appeared to have only recently hit puberty. She played the fiddle. And finally, towering over them both by about a foot was a boy playing a single maraca. Something about his eyes implied that he wasn't quite right, but it didn't affect his playing one bit. He just shook and shook that maraca like it was what he had been born to do.

At the doorway, I spotted a familiar face. It was Tracey, my new roommate. As usual, her outfit appeared to be freshly pressed and her curly hair reflected the lights above as if varnished. She handed me a chapel card, an index card that documented one's compulsory attendance at chapel. Administered by the chapel chicks at the beginning of chapel and then collected by the same at the doors at the end of chapel, these cards represented an airtight system of attendance regulation...just begging to be circumvented by the industrious.

Tracey was a "chapel chick." The job of "chapel chick" at my university was for the more progressive womyn of the school. Like holy club bouncers, chapel chicks monitor the doors of the auditorium and take roll of all who enter there. Because of their elevated stature and position in the public eye, chapel chicks must conduct themselves appropriately at all times—both on and off campus. At my school, this necessarily meant making sure that they represented their school well by speaking kindly to people, not using foul language, and making sure that their pedicures were perfect.

Tracey shot me an ivory white smile as she passed me a chapel card.

"He's over there," she informed me over the music, nodding toward a blond head sticking about a foot over the others in a nearby pew. "He asked me to let y'all know."

I gave her a nod of thanks, choosing not to get hung up on her persistence in referring to me in the plural, and headed over to where Scott had saved a seat for me.

On the other side of me sat Karen, a girl who lived on the floor above me and with whom I had been fostering a friendship. Although from Texas, Karen seemed about as turned off by the whole fluff and spray culture as I did. Short, blonde, and predisposed to the use of a bandana on her head to which she referred as her thinking cap, Karen struck me from the beginning as a genuine person. Add to that the fact that she was funny and intelligent, and I was pretty sure that I had found the person who would be my best friend for the next four years.

Karen shot me a wry smile and nudged me on the arm.

"Thought you weren't coming," she told me.

"As if," I snorted back.

Just then, Pastor Smart supernovaed onto the stage with mike in hand and began belting out the words to the song his family was playing: *If God is for us, who can be against us?* Soon, the entire congregation of college students was on its feet singing along. With the Smart Family Band in the lead, we tore through hymn after hymn, clapping and singing for nearly half an hour. When we finally sat down, we were exhausted and sweaty. A couple of the wilting chapel chicks had opened a few windows near the back, through which they were attempting to suck the life back into their perfectly applied cheeks and rosebud lips.

"Sex!" Yelled Pastor Smart from the stage, startling us all into attention, "is a beautiful thing." He looked around at us, ludicrously daring anybody to contradict him in the looming silence, broken only by the static shock of a dropped maraca somewhere on the stage behind him. A burst of adrenalin had risen to my chest with the unexpected yelp of the word that was the culmination of my heart's desire. I think Scott grabbed my hand.

"Say it with me now, 'Sex...is a beautiful thing.'" We repeated after him, hesitantly at first, and then with more gusto. Soon, the entire student body was chanting the mantra he had given us. Some even stomped their feet to it. One of the basketball players behind me shouted it out with all his might.

Then we stopped. He pressed the microphone up to his mouth and spoke in a low, booming voice:

"But only in the proper context."

We all watched Pastor Smart, now pacing back and forth across the stage as he formulated what was coming next. Oh, how he had our attention then. He took a turn by the pulpit, back to the piano, jogged back to the center, bounced in place for a crescendoing eight count, and then erupted with, "AND THAT PROPER CONTEXT IS WITHIN THE CONTEXT GOD PLANNED FOR US—A HOLY, LOVE-FILLED, GODLY MARRIAGE AS DEMONSTRATED TO US BY HIS LOVE FOR THE CHURCH!" His hands were raised, people were whispering amens, a few people were crying.

"Everybody, I want you to do something with me."

Eagerly, we awaited our orders.

"Look to your left, look to your right...your future mate, might be in sight."

With smiles on our faces, we did as we were told. Even so, Scott and I did not look around too eagerly.

For the next twenty minutes, we listened in rapt attention to Pastor Smart's plan for a godly and lasting marriage—a plan, which as far as I could tell, mostly involved not doing it before we said 'I do'. By the time he was panting, exhausted over the pulpit Salvador Dali style, we weren't ready for him to stop. We needed more. We had so many questions.

Almost prophetically, he seemed to understand this. At his cue, the ends of the pews were suddenly flanked by chapel chicks, their Skin So Soft arms heavily laden with stacks of cards. At first, I thought it might be time to hand in our chapel attendance cards, and I scrambled to dig mine out from my back pocket where I had put it for safe-keeping. But no, it was something else. They were coming down the pews now. When the stack came to me, I grabbed one off the top, hungrily studying the wallet-sized wisdom Pastor Smart had prepared for us.

At the top of the card was printed the words "Smart Chart," followed by a list of acceptable activities in which young Christian men and women could engage, as well as a list of unacceptable activities. The activities themselves were color coded and ranged from green to red. Hand holding, of course, was at the top of the list over the color green, followed by hugging. Closed mouth kissing was next on the list, superimposed over a kind of yellowish-green, with open mouthed kissing following close behind it. By the bright yellow color of the chart, however, you could see that open-mouthed kissing was crossing into some sort of danger zone, which was followed directly by heavy petting and oral sex placed in boxes of orange and reddish orange, respectively. At the bottom, enveloped in call girl red, was the word "intercourse," so that we knew without a shadow of a doubt that this was a slap in God's face and would lead ultimately to one's eternal demise.

A prayer was initiated. In the background, the piano softly played "Just As I Am." Pastor Smart mopped the distinguished brow under his immoveable hair. People began coming down to the altar in droves.

It was soon after this that the mike was opened up to testimonies. Pastor Smart was there to challenge us, after all. Was there anyone out there who could offer a word of encouragement? How was God working in our lives? Was God moving anybody to speak? Would anybody like to *share*? This takes honesty, people.

The first person to the mike was a diminutive girl whom I recognized from the cafeteria. She usually wore a white smock and had a giant scoop in one hand, but I could tell it was her.

"I just wanted to say that there is so much pressure out there and it's good to have people to stand strong with you. Thank you, Pastor Smart."

A smattering of applause.

Another person approached the mike—a guy, red hair, pale-faced.

"My brother had sex and got," he paused as a wave of emotion washed over him, "a *venerable* disease. God punished him for his sin, but it's not too late for you. Y'all should listen to Pastor Smart. He's really...I don't know."

Pastor Smart nodded, smiling knowingly.

Next up, a boy I recognized from my Fine Arts class. He's tall, curly-haired, terrified.

"I'm just...." He looks out over the audience, starts to lose his nerve. His face has gone an eerie shade of pale.

"Go on," says Pastor Smart, "it's OK. You're among friends here."

"It's just that, I've done," he pauses again.

"It's OK," says our speaker, "you're among friends. There is no judgment here. We have all sinned and fallen short. God has forgiven you."

"No, I need to say it. I need to confess."

Pastor Smart nods; begins moving towards him.

"It's just that, I've had this struggle for so long. I've tried to stop, but I can't."

Karen grabs my arm. I look over at her blankly.

"I—I keep asking for help to stop. It's that thing guys do."

"OK," says Pastor Smart laughing mildly, now trying to intervene. He begins reaching out for the microphone.

Oh my goodness, I think to myself, realizing where he's headed. But he's on a derailed train headed for a cliff.

Sit down, somebody yells out. *You don't have to—*

Finally, he blurts it out.

"I can't stop...*masturbating*. There, I said it. I can't stop! I'm an addict!" He breaks down into a fit of sobs. Quickly, several people rush him off the stage. Pastor Smart grabs the mike, says something unintelligible. We all sit there in numb shock. A few guys in the back are already making wisecracks. Chapel is dismissed.

Nobody knew what would happen next. There was a rumor that he had been placed on suicide watch. What he ended up doing was condemning himself to certain social death—one which would end up following him around the country as he changed schools a total of three times.

*

Sexuality in any form is a tricky and charged subject in the Evangelical world. Before marriage, during marriage, outside of marriage. For some people it has to do with the commitment of it, for others it has to do with the purpose of it, and for still others it simply has to do with the pleasure of it.

The phrase "sexual immorality" in the Bible has developed to include all things sexual outside of marriage within the Evangelical church: premarital and extramarital sex, and yes, sometimes even masturbation. Most people seem to accept this as fact without ever stopping to really ask if that is actually what it means. Perhaps it is referring to temple prostitution. Perhaps it is referring to rape or incest. Perhaps it is referring to adultery. Incidentally, adultery meant something entirely different back then than it does today as it could only be considered adultery if it involved a man (married or not) having sex with a married woman. It was not considered adultery if a married man had sex with an unmarried woman. The nuance lay in the marital status of the woman, as she was another man's property. The point is, what "sexual immorality" actually meant is difficult to distinguish. It is, at the very least, debatable.

No matter where a person sits on their interpretation of sexual immorality, though, when they are convinced that what they have done is wrong—and that they can't stop—then they are now in the position of anguished, all-consuming guilt. Doing something wrong leads to Hell, they are told. And when faced with Hell, confessing to an auditorium filled with college students that you can't stop touching yourself doesn't seem like such a bad idea.

And who can blame him? We had been told a million times that this world is not what matters. It might not even be entirely real. It was the salvation of his own soul that mattered. He only took this to its logical conclusion.

Dwayne's World

People go to great measures to break with their routines in order to disappoint their families en route to sitting in God's palm: they pray, starve themselves, jump in glacier water, crawl for miles on their knees.

A Danish friend of mine spent several months rotating religious groups on this quest. When I first met him, he informed me that he had spent time with "the Evangelicals," so he sort of understood where I was coming from. He had also spent time with the Hari Krishnas and the Moonies, although he did admit that he was somewhat compelled by the offering of free food. After we departed ways two years later, he would live several months in a Shaolin monastery where he worked his muscles to the bone from dawn until dusk running all over the place and balancing on posts. He spent nearly a quarter of his time convincing people to please not spit on the floor of his room. People crowded the doorway every time he had to relieve himself. Watch the tall, big-nosed, hairy white man take a poo. Very entertaining, I'm told.

But enlightenment is worth it, isn't it? How can truth be found if it is not sought outside of one's comfort zone?

My own search led me at one point to travel alone to Europe. I went to England. Denmark. I took a train through

Spain. In Sevilla, I walked the damp January streets through piles of fallen oranges and thought about life. The mistakes I had made. The mistakes I still needed to make.

The oranges were so thick on the sidewalks that I began to feel dizzy as I maneuvered my way through them, so when I nearly ran headfirst into a Spanish gypsy, it took me quite by surprise. It would be much later when I realized that I was walking along one of the walls of one of the world's oldest and largest cathedrals and home to the tomb of Christopher Columbus. But that meant nothing to me at that moment with my eyes on the ground, scanning and plotting my path through scattered orange fruit.

The woman locked eyes with me. She was middle-aged with creases around her eyes that betrayed a lifetime of bright sunlight and cigarette smoke. Wild black hair ran down her back like a mane. Her long, green skirt bore a dangerously high slit up the front and was paired with a navy blazer that unapologetically belonged with a different outfit altogether. In her hand, she held out a small sprig of herbs to me. I noticed all of these

Guide to Churchese

Cult – 1. In sociological terms, a cult is a fringe religion led by a manipulative leader who has immense power over his or her group. One well-known example is Jim Jones' Peoples Temple, based in Guyana before the mass 'suicide' of approximately 900 people due mostly to laced Flavor-aid. 2. In Evangelical terms, any religious group that claims to be Christian, but that does not accept the "historical" Christian doctrines (Jesus saves, virgin birth, Trinity, etc.). By this definition, Evangelicals consider the Church of Jesus Christ of Latter Day Saints (Mormons) and the Jehovah's Witnesses to be cults. Wicca and Buddhism are not considered to be cults, because they do not claim to be Christian.

things only vaguely and reached out to take the herbs from
her as if caught in a spell. Then she began to speak rapidly in
Spanish that I could barely keep up with—about my past, my
present, my future. She spoke fervently and I watched her tell
my fortune as if I were watching myself, as well. She reached
out and put her hand over my heart. I flinched only a little.

"Su corazón es fuerte," she told me, and then stopped.
Your heart is strong. We stared into each other's eyes—a stare that
stopped time. She removed her hand from my chest and took
my hand, the hand with the herbs she had given me.

"Para su protecciòn," she said piercingly, her eyes boring
deep into my soul. I barely even noticed myself handing her a
couple of euros.

And then she was gone, leaving me alone to stand amongst
the crowds of people wandering along the busy Avenida
Constituciòn. After a while, a young man who had been
watching me on the street corner took me to be a lost tourist
and politely approached me.

"Puedo ayudarle?" he asked. He was handsome and wore
well-polished shoes. I looked down at the herbs the gypsy had
left with me before meeting his eyes.

"No. No gracias," I told him. *I'm fine.* I looked around
my surroundings as if I were in a dream. Surfaces I normally
regarded as solid seemed to slip around and through me.

"Me llamo Paulo," he said, holding out his hand to me.

When I reached out to take his hand I felt almost as if his
skin were a part of mine.

A smile then broke across his face like a Picasso sky. Then,
he leaned forward and kissed me on the cheek. I watched him
do it as if it were the most normal thing in the world for a
stranger to kiss me on the cheek while I stood on a street corner
amidst crowds and oranges and fortune-telling gypsies.

Watching my expression, Paulo laughed before clutching both hands to his heart and abruptly disappearing down the street into the crowd.

Su corazón es fuerte, she had told me.

And then she was gone.

*

I did not mean to join a cult. It happened accidentally, which is to say that it happened in the usual way, I suppose. I do not imagine most people who become involved with cults do so with intention. But I missed my Youth Group. More specifically, I missed my leaders. I missed Pastor Mark...and I missed King Richard.

No matter how much I had mentally prepared myself for the fact that Scott and I would be on our own and could no longer rely on him as our spiritual leader at college, I wasn't ready. Richard was special to us. Who had been there for us every time the evils of the world threatened to drag us down? Richard. Who had shown us by example what being "in the world and not of the world" meant by converting one soul at a time over club soda and darts at his neighborhood bar? Who had taught me that there is no shame in toting one's Bible to the hair salon so that I might be an inspiration to my gay hair stylist? And who had taught me that life is like a checkbook, which can only be balanced properly if God is in the equation? Richard, Richard, and Richard.

What was it about him? How could one man be so inspiring? Sure, he was at least 10 years older than us, but he was cool, nonetheless. Carelessly cool and righteously radical. Everywhere we went, I thought I saw him. Every time I would see a Hyundai drive by campus—an occurrence which happened more frequently than you might think—I would find myself trying desperately to get a glimpse of the driver.

The void our separation had left was crippling. The absence of his regular guidance both stunted and bewildered us. We were like a blind man reaching for a glass of water who gets a glass of pureed raw fish, instead. We were lost without him. We were subjects without a king.

In absentia of our glorious leader, the scepter fell to Dwayne, a janitor in the science building, which is how Scott met him. Dwayne was busily sanitizing urinals and Scott had just finished up his third coffee of the morning, so you could say their relationship was one born out of a codependency from the very beginning.

Often when I would go to meet Scott after class, I would find Scott and Dwayne walking the long halls together, sometimes with Scott even taking a turn at the broom. Dwayne, a tall man with a peppery beard and droopy lids, would look at me when I caught him at it and shrug.

"He insisted," he would say with lids half shut while reaching over and giving one of Scott's shoulders a grateful squeeze.

Later, when I questioned Scott about it, he explained somewhat fiercely, "I don't suppose you think I'm too good to push a broom, do you? Do you think Jesus would be too good to push a broom?"

If Scott wanted to befriend the guy who cleaned up the formaldehyde-and-blood-smeared floors, and perhaps the occasional monkey feces, I didn't see what business it was of mine.

But as it turned out, there was much more to Dwayne than met the eye. During those long walks up and down the hallways, winding past the iguana cages, with the occasional, yet brief, foray into the cadaver lab, Scott learned that Dwayne did not have to be a janitor. Rather, he had carefully chosen his current profession specifically for its deprecation value. It was all part of his spiritual journey. He would make himself as lowly as possible, so that he could understand the mind of Jesus better.

As a matter of fact, Dwayne the Janitor claimed to have made a series of rather impressive inventions in his day— before he signed up to clean the toilets of those who dissected frog bladders for a living. Among them were the Heads Up Display, in use on Air Force jets; a satellite tracking system; and the Num Lock button on the computer keyboard, despite other people having taken the credit for them. Had it been a few years later, he would have beaten Gore to the Internet.

"This guy knows what he's talking about," Scott told me later. "And he's as fed up with the establishment as we are."

The "establishment" to which he was referring was the "cultural" church. As we had learned from Richard, this was supposed to be in direct opposition to the "real" church, which involved people like us who had tired of going through the motions of religion and were seeking an authentic experience with Jesus Christ. We wanted a church that was a little less rule-bound and we wanted authenticity. Thus, with the scene set for our grand rebellion, we agreed to meet Dwayne the Janitor at his apartment one night for a Bible study—just a gathering of other true believers who were tired of selling out to the establishment of organized religion. It was to be unlike any Bible study we had ever seen.

I was used to seeing Dwayne in a shabby pair of blue coveralls and a large ring of keys around his wrist, so it was with some measure of surprise when I met him at his apartment door that first time and he was wearing a V-neck sweater and something that looked suspiciously like a cravat. I had heard that his daughter went to our school, so I was disappointed when I didn't see her there that night. But I quickly decided that I didn't care. He was so warm and friendly. He gave Scott an enormous hug, but he didn't so much as touch me, which only served to prove that he was a real gentleman. It wasn't until later in the evening that I realized that the thing I had mistaken for a cravat was actually one of those turtleneck dickey inserts that had come up and bunched itself around his neck. Also, I noticed for the first time at that close proximity that he had that old man smell you get in thrift stores, but that just made him all the more real.

His wife, Darlene, a demure woman with long gray hair, passed around a platter of treats involving various combinations of chocolate chips, marshmallows, pretzels and canned cheese before withdrawing to a chair in the corner. This was apparently just the cue for which he had been waiting. He pulled out an old guitar from behind the plastic protected sofa and led us in a few of the older styled hymns—hymns like "I Know that My Redeemer Lives," "Blessed Assurance," and "I Sent You to Reap." In any other setting, I would have thought these a tad old-fashioned, but in the context of the highly progressive circumstances in which we had gathered, I could see that these were, in fact, revolutionary choices.

Most of the Bible studies I had attended lately focused on the more modern choruses in an attempt to relate to us, the new generation. But we were tired of *being related to*. After all, we had left the protected borders of King Richard and had found the lords of our new land to be sad imposters of the original. We didn't care how loud the speakers were in the college room at the church next to us. The leader there just couldn't pull off U2's "40" like Richard could. And when they sang "Swing

Low Sweet Chariot," the entire college group looked at us like we were crazy when we called out in the appropriate place, "I saw a band of CHICKENS coming after me" instead of their comparably feathered heavenly counterparts.

But with Dwayne, things were different. Armed with nothing more than a beat up old acoustic and a smudged pair of bifocals so that he could read the chord progressions he had scrawled out earlier on a used Chick-fil-A napkin, he showed us the beauty in the old ways. We sang for nearly an hour, and by the time we were finished it was as if we had been baptized anew and saw for the first time with open eyes.

He talked to us for the next hour on the topic of being a "true" Christian, a subject which resonated well with us. Our heads bobbed up and down throughout as we agreed with what Dwayne was saying. He spoke of an established church that had sold out to modern culture. Of political battles amongst pastors. Of the tendency of churches to construct unnecessary rule systems in line with their interpretation. What did the true church need any of that for, he challenged. The Bible was crystal clear, he told us holding up a copy of a King James Version Bible. Who needs a newfangled, Harvard bred interpretation? The Bible was its own interpreter. And our hearts the open vessel. "I am the way, the truth and the life," he reminded us at the end. Jesus was the way to God, not the church.

At the end, when Darlene passed around an offering plate, we didn't hesitate. It didn't even seem weird or out of place that it was an *actual* offering plate: as in, a felt lined, wooden plate complete with a wide rim for ease of handling. We just doled out whatever green stuff we happened to be carrying in the remote creases of our freshman pockets, and were even pleased to thank them for the opportunity on the way out.

For the next few months we saw a lot of Dwayne and Darlene. Sometimes we would meet during the day on campus under trees on the grass. We would pray and sing to the accompaniment of his guitar while our fellow students passed by and wondered how they, too, could someday achieve such a level of spirituality. And we would not have dreamed of missing a meeting at his apartment on Thursday nights. I don't know what it was—I think we were just so proud that we were really thinking through the issues. We weren't mindlessly going through the motions and showing up to church each Sunday like everybody else. We were *radical* Christians. Richard—and Jesus, of course—would have been so proud. Each time that offering plate was passed around, we were eager to prove just how much that ministry meant to us, too.

At some point we developed a bad taste in our mouth for the church we were attending on Sundays, and stopped going, taking jobs in a church nursery instead. The congregation was just so lukewarm. Not like us, so completely *on-fire*. My parents were a bit annoyed by the whole thing, so I solved that little problem. I stopped calling them so much.

It was at this point that Scott and I started receiving little gifts in the mail, a pattern we would soon come to recognize whenever our parents thought we were backsliding into a life of sin and impending, eternal doom. At first, it was just the little things: cheerful little notes saying that they were praying for us, bookmarks with the Christian interpretation of our names, bulletins from our home church with notes in the margins from the previous Sunday.... I thought it was cute at first.

"Aw! They miss us!" I told Scott. He screwed up his face at me.

"No, they're worried about us."

"What do you mean? Why?" This was certainly news to me. Why should they be worried about us? We had never been so right with Jesus in our lives. We had even put the kibosh on some of our more favorite couple activities, choosing to stop at a simple goodnight kiss as we actively practiced purity so that we would be all the more righteous—greenish-yellow on "The Smart Chart," but several color progressions above the danger zone. And it was worth it. Never before had we felt like things were so good. For the first time in my life, I *knew* my direction. All of the questions I'd had before seemed to be laid to rest. Dwayne had all the answers.

"They think we've joined a cult," Scott explained.

"Who? Dwayne and Darlene's church?" I was completely blown away by this bit of information. If anyone knew what a cult was, it was most certainly me. My dad could fill a wing of the Library of Congress with the books he had on various cults, so I had read a thing or two. As a Sunday School teacher, he was practically famous for what he called "cult month," which made a regular appearance in his curriculum each year.

Suffice it to say that I was quite conversant on the topic by the time I met Dwayne. I became all the more resolute. I began inviting friends.

My best girlfriend at the time, Karen, was so touched by the invitation that she could barely look me in the eye. I believe she was trying not to cry.

"I've seen you guys around campus singing and stuff," she admitted.

I knew it! She had totally been keeping an envious eye on us. I recognized that I had been a little scarce those days. Before we met Dwayne, she and I had always eaten lunch together in the school cafeteria. Like Scott, she was a science major and would usually come over with him after class. But how could

I make time for lunch every day when there were people for whom I needed to pray? What about all the godless children in China?

"They aren't just *literally* starving, you know," I pointed out to her when I had finished explaining my rationale as to why I had ditched her and practically forgotten her name.

Karen looked surprised by that and met my eyes for the first time. As she was in the middle of studying, she wore her long blonde hair back in her thinking cap. She nervously tucked back a piece of hair that had fallen into her face as she stood to her feet. Clearly, her impulse was to go. She had no idea what to do with the revelation I had given her. It was that powerful.

"You should join us," I told her, resting my hand on her shoulder. "We could pray for the god-starved children of China *together*."

She mumbled something to the effect that she would think about it, and I just knew I had won her over. For Christ, that is. Certainly not for me. And definitely not for Dwayne and Darlene. A *cult*! Bah!

She never did show up to any of our meetings. As a matter of fact, I was beginning to get the impression that she was avoiding me. Bothered by this, I decided to confront her head-on in the lunch line.

"Oh, hey, Karen. I didn't see you there," I said cheerily.

She smiled knowingly at me.

"How's your day going?"

"Fine," she said cautiously, grabbing a bowl of orange gelatin off the metal rack.

"Doing anything later this afternoon?"

"Why? You want me to come to one of your meetings?"

I acted surprised.

"No! I just wanted to know if you wanted to go get something to drink at the café with me."

"Does it involve Kool-Aid?"

I crossed my arms in front of my chest.

"No. It just so happens that it does not."

She stopped in the middle of pulling some sort of jiggly plate full of saucy chicken over noodles onto her tray.

"I'm sorry. But it's just that I'm not interested."

"But why?" I asked, incredulous that she had so firmly made up her mind about something that she knew nothing. "We have such a great time just singing and praying together. Why wouldn't you want to be a part of that?"

"Look, there's someone I think you should talk to. Why don't you meet me in my room this afternoon at 3?"

Later that afternoon, I arrived to find her in her room, as promised. To my surprise, Beth was sitting on Karen's bed.

"You're Dwayne's daughter!" I smiled, excitedly.

She rolled her eyes.

"Right. Dwayne's daughter." Her voice was dripping with sarcasm.

I scrunched my eyebrows at her.

"What?"

I looked back and forth between her and Karen.

"You might as well tell her," Karen encouraged her.

Beth sighed.

"Dwayne's not my father. But he would kill me if he knew I told you."

I was confused.

"Why does he say he's your father if he's not your—"

"You mean other than the God complex?"

My jaw dropped wide. How could she be saying such a thing about our leader? My leader!

"My mom and I moved in with him four years ago. We were practically living on the streets. They got married and now he insists I call him 'Daddy' in front of everyone. It's a big show. He doesn't want anyone to know."

She went on to tell me about what a control freak he was in her life.

"Do you know that he chooses my lipstick color? And if I wear a shirt with the shoulder seam that's not straight up and down, I'm in huge trouble. He says that the shirt's too big."

I was incredulous. That didn't sound anything at all like the freedom from rules he was preaching. He was like Mommy Dearest with a penis and a mop.

"But, how can this be?"

"God complex." She and Karen finished the sentence in unison. She must have seen that I was having trouble with that one, because she raised her eyebrows at me.

"Haven't you noticed how he ends every service with that whole, 'I am the way, the truth and the life' thing? Did you think he was talking about *Jesus*?"

I just stared at her, horrified.

"He thinks he's the second coming or whatever. Just wait until you hear how he intends to reveal himself."

Scott and I went back to one more meeting before backing out altogether. Having been tipped off by Beth, we began to notice all manner of little comments that we had not really paid attention to before. Statements like, "we are the true church, nobody else seems to get it" and "some of you will have to leave your families behind in order to follow my teaching."

When Dwayne realized that we were not going to come back, he became cold to Scott, certainly no longer stopping to chit chat with him in the Science building, and definitely no more taking turns at the broom. Over the course of the next month, Scott observed him becoming more and more agitated in his presence until one day he just disappeared. His daughter, too, had left the school.

Slowly, things on the surface went back to normal. Without Dwayne to stand in the way, Karen and I were able to repair our somewhat strained relationship. I started calling my parents again. The gifts in the mail stopped. I even began to make appearances back at the college group at the church, although admittedly without much zeal.

But something had changed.

Razed and Confused

I AM A HUGE FAN OF FERMENTATION. THERE ARE FEW THINGS I enjoy more than a glass of red wine on an evening with friends. Especially Merlot. Yeah, that's right I said it. Despite the best efforts of the writers of the film *Sideways*, I am still in love with the "M word." Give me a glass with a nice bowl to roll it around in and I am one happy chick. And while I am not an addict by any means, I have come to look forward to this experience with at least some measure of regularity. For me, the hardest part of pregnancy was not the back pain, difficulty of sleep—or even the labor. No, it is the necessity to cut back from that sublime burgundy in the glass.

Unlike most of my peers within the church in which I grew up, I was not taught by my parents that the drinking of alcohol is a sin. Rather, my training was of a more subtle nature. It wasn't that drinking alcohol itself was a sin—unless of course it crossed over to drunkenness, at which point it ranked fairly highly amongst the seven deadliest. It was more that drinking in front of somebody else who might be inclined to have a problem with it was. This is a nuance that I would not expect the average person who did not grow up under these circumstances to readily understand, so suffice it to say that my comfort factor with drinking was almost nil.

It probably goes without saying that alcohol was a scarcity at my house. My parents reserved the drinking of alcohol for situations in which a cultural discomfort needed to be avoided. Specifically, this meant that while drinking socially at parties was a no-no on account of the possibility that it might encourage some weak soul to tip the scales toward the inclination to don a lampshade, drinking with foreigners in the privacy of one's home or overseas was an acceptable—and even necessary—activity. Because, presumably, foreigners would be irreparably offended should one explain that one doesn't drink.

Guide to Churchese

Sinning – Evangelicals see the act of sinning as the willful disobedience of God. So, sin never occurs without a conscious or willful decision, which is really sweet because most of the bad things I do are really just stupid mistakes. Can I hear an 'amen' somebody?

I was 14 when I first tasted alcohol. I had only recently celebrated my birthday when my family went on vacation to the United Kingdom. It was Chevy Chase in a rented car with suitcases hanging out the windows and the whole works. We had just spent a harrowing couple of days with Dad negotiating the left side of the street when we stopped by the grace of God in one piece at Stratford-Upon-Avon, home of Shakespeare and a boy named Shandy.

Now, Shandy and his friends were cute, and my two sisters and I found an excuse to pal around with them for the better part of one of the days we were there. When my sisters and I arrived back late to the hostel to find Mom and Dad leaning meaningfully on their elbows out the window, we cast our infraction in light of having spent a valuable day gaining a cultural education. In the process, I let it drop that we had met—it was the funniest thing—a guy, *some boy really*, named Shandy who showed us all around the bless'd land o' Shakespeare in his car with a few of his friends—and *how lucky were we?* Unbelievably, it worked. Encouraged by the insight into a different culture that his girls had received, my father, the holder of the keys to higher education, took it upon himself to add his own lesson: the meaning of Shandy's name.

With his nose hot on the trail of an "educational moment," Dad marched us all, women-and-children, the very next day to the nearest pub where he promptly bought us one. To share. With the five of us huddled around a table in the heart of Merry Old England, we passed around a single pint: half beer, half lemonade.

We kept the bender in England on the down-low from our friends. As Mom and Dad had pointed out on the way back from the airport, they might not understand. If they found out that we had partaken of alcohol, it might encourage them, too, to experiment and before we could blink, half of my class at the Christian school would be living in the gutter and drinking from paper bags as they slid slowly downhill toward the fiery lake. Did we want that kind of responsibility?

Over the years, I would watch as Mom and Dad would host various guests from Germany, Russia, and beyond. If they would bring a bottle of wine to our house as a gift, it would be opened at dinner and passed around appropriately in our long-stem water glasses, reserved just for the occasion. We did not want to cause an international incident, after all. We were ambassadors for Christ.

*

And so I left for college, taking with me two valuable lessons from all of this. First, if you're going to drink, drink alone.

And second, for the love of Pete, don't TELL anybody about it. So when Scott's roommate got nailed for his indiscretion, I could only shake my head.

Freddie was a music major from rural Oklahoma where he had grown up in a trailer home with his mom and nine brothers. According to him, there was a hole in the bottom of the trailer through which he and his brothers derived hours of fun throwing rocks at whatever small rodents happened to be passing underneath. He had arrived at our college with only a duffel bag and a dream: he was going to become a music minister.

Over the weeks and months that were to follow, it became obvious that he and Scott were just about as opposite as you can imagine. Scott was tidy; Freddie was not. Scott was tall and blond; Freddie was stocky with thick, dark hair covering his entire body and feet like a Hobbit. Scott played games and wrote programs on his computer; Freddie was confounded by the electric typewriter. Scott kept a bowl of fruit on his desk; Freddie kept a jar of pickled pigs feet.

But despite their differences, Scott liked Freddie. As a person, Freddie could not have been more giving. He had a heart that was as big as a barn *and* a silo. If ever Scott needed anything that Freddie could help out with, Freddie was there for him in a flash. So when after two months into our freshman year I met Freddie coming down the stairs from the dining hall with one eyebrow missing, I was concerned.

"What happened to Freddie?" I asked Scott when I caught up with him inside. As usual, he was helping himself to a bowl of cereal over by the giant dispensers. It did not matter what time of day it was. If it was mealtime, it was cereal time.

"Yeah, about that..." He paused before pulling the lever to the milk machine. He looked sideways at me.

"What did you do?" I narrowed my eyes at him.

"It wasn't just me," he informed me, biting his lip. "Things might have gotten a little out of control."

I followed him over to a table. It turned out that Freddie had returned late the previous night in an altered state. According to what they pieced together that morning from an infuriated, yet penitent Freddie, it had been his first time. He had gone out with a friend, got loaded up on light beer in the parking lot of the Taco Bell down the street, and in the process managed to lose all memory of anything that followed. Miraculously, he managed to haul himself up the stairs of the dormitory and into his own bed, where he proceeded to puke up the contents of two six-packs, along with a bean burrito and half of a tostada. By the time Scott arrived barefoot on the darkened spongy scene, Freddie was passed out cold in the midst of his own filth, and the room was sprayed down like a set from *The Exorcist*.

Forced into the hall by a smell reminiscent of a sewer back-up in the men's restroom at a Phish concert, Scott knocked on the door of his nearest neighbors in request of sanctuary. But it could not be so simple.

Once the guys next door caught wind of what had happened—both from Scott and through the ventilation system—it was a free for all. In a matter of minutes, a virtual lynching mob had shown up outside of Scott and Freddie's door armed with all manner of sharp and dangerous objects.

But their goal was not to hurt him. That would have been almost kind in comparison. Instead, their idea was to *punish* him. Slowly, stealthily, they crept into the putrid room, took off all of Freddie's clothes as he floated in the murky pond of his alcohol-induced coma...and shaved him. *Half* of him, that is.

When they were done with his furry back, they carefully rolled him over, lathered him up with shaving cream and shaved the front side. One arm, one leg, half of his chest, one foot—and yes, even half of his manly glory. Half of his mustache and the one eyebrow were the last to go. It would be like taking a black bear and razing him down halfway until he was something akin to a small hippo. Or, half of a small hippo. Whatever it was, though, it was not pretty.

By this point, the entire dormitory had heard what had happened and everyone who was in the building had paraded through the room to get a better look. It was only a matter of time before the Resident Director became involved.

Like I've said before, drinking at our college was a punishable offense as it was out of step with our church's image of a Christ-centered, holy life. Our church had even gone so far as to call drinking a "sin" based on a few verses concerning drunkenness and foolishness. Never mind the fact that the Bible actually shows Jesus providing *more* wine for a wedding party once it had run out. Capital guy, in my book. If I ran into him at a bar, I'd totally buy him a round.

Whatever the case, our school had its own opinion on that matter: godly men and women don't drink, and it was the administration's job to turn out godly men and women to the world. Men and women who could represent Christ in an appropriate way. Adults who could think for themselves and choose righteousness in the midst of a darkened world. Bright, young, responsible men and women of God.

"Go to your rooms!", snapped the RD when he discovered Freddie spread out on his bed like Aslan on the stone table. "Go on, git! I'll call your mothers if I have to."

The boys of Snow Hall scattered like mice, escaping through the nearest available crevices and stairwells.

The RD looked at Freddie, half-shaved and comatose on his bed in a sea of shaving cream and shook his head.

"I have to report this," he told Scott, the only one to remain behind from the mass exodus. It was, after all, his room. There was nowhere to hide.

The next morning, Freddie was summoned from his sleep to stand before the administration with neither sunglasses nor aspirin for comfort. Within an hour, it was decided that, as public as the situation was, there was no choice but to make an example of him. He would have to submit to the fate of all who crossed that line and were discovered drinking while enrolled at the university. He would be tried as an adult and he would have to face the consequences of sinning against God and the administration. After they called his mommy, he was given a one-week suspension and promptly enrolled in Alcoholics Anonymous.

Freddie did eventually manage to forgive Scott for his role in the loss of his pride. Although Scott had not actually laid a hand on a single razor that night, he had been the link that exposed him to the scrutiny and judgment of all. It took a couple of weeks into the program, but he was eventually able to face what had happened to him with some measure of good humor and finally shaved the other eyebrow to match, as well as the other half of his mustache. He even came and joined us at the table in the dining hall a couple of times while he went over the steps from his AA group.

Needless to say, Freddie never touched another drop of liquid barley again. He had learned from his disobedience. I, on the other hand, walked away with a different lesson.

To begin with, most of those guys who went to such efforts of stripping Freddie of any whisker of dignity were no angels. Quite a few of them were known to sneak off any night of the week and come back a little buzzed. Screw the rules, these guys were going to have their college experience. And similar to the likes of me and Ted Haggard, they were going to do it out of the public eye...and they certainly were not going to *tell* anybody about it. Because once they did that, they opened themselves up to the very same judgment that they themselves were doling out.

So, Now What?

It is amazing what sounds like a good idea at the age of 19: 3 A.M. Dennys, bungee jumping, car camping trips to Tijuana, all night bar crawls with a fake id...or, in my case, marriage.

Don't misunderstand me—I love my husband—but how I could have chosen an early start at sewing curtain valances and balancing our humble joint checking account over, say, backpacking across Europe with my friends over the summer, I cannot fully grasp in retrospect.

Of course, I blame the Youth Group. Every other talk we listened to as teens had involved how exciting married sex would be and how much it was worth waiting for.

Married sex. While it truly does seem to get better by the year, nobody told us at that point that we would have to work at it to make it so. That we would have to get creative if we wanted to keep the spice in our relationship. You know, think outside the box while at the same time occasionally pulling certain props out of said box. I think I had the idea that because we waited to have real sex until our wedding night that God would bless us with a lifetime of uninterrupted passion and easy orgasms.

Regardless, we knew two things at the ripe age of 19. One: we wanted to have sex. Two: premarital sex was wrong. Thinking about it was wrong. Planning for it was wrong. And doing it was definitely wrong. We were supposed to be hot for God, not each other. There was only one way around it: Marriage.

In marriage, we could stop feeling guilty for all of those crazy, out of control desires that sent us parking in a steamed over car at the edge of the Nature Reserve night after night.

Yes, Oklahoma has a nature reserve.

When we told Pastor Mark over the phone of our plans to get married after our freshman year of college, he was practically moved to

Guide to Churchese

Marriage – 1. The state in which an Evangelical may finally engage 'legally' in sex. 2. The state in which most Evangelical teenagers move from idealism to realism.

tears. In the background, we could hear Deb cheering over the television. After as long as we had waited, he said, we were finally going to find out what it was all about.

"But don't blow it now," he cautioned us after a brief interrogation to make sure that we had remained pure while away at college, "you're so close and you're going to be tempted to seal the deal early. Don't give in now. You're almost at the end of the marathon."

What he perhaps should have mentioned but didn't was that we were about to end one marathon and begin another.

"There was a couple once," he began, his voice suddenly taking on a melodic tone, "who were two days away from their wedding. Everyone in their family was out making preparations, leaving them home alone together. Now, they had stayed pure for each other, but something about the proximity of the wedding made them forget their vows to the Lord. One thing led to another, and the two found themselves without clothes.

He lifted her to carry her upstairs to the bedroom when all of a sudden, they ran into her mother at the top of the stairs. They did not realize she was home. He dropped his beloved fiancée down the flight of stairs, she broke her leg, and she had to wear a cast to the wedding."

"Why was her mother home?" I whispered.

"So wait. You must wait. But marriage—*wow*—you won't regret it."

My father, on the other hand, did not agree. He thought we should wait until graduation. As far as he was concerned, we should be waiting even a lot longer.

"When you are up there on that platform saying I do, you may be distracted by an annoying squeak," he told us while we were home over Christmas break, "That will be the sound of me turning off the money faucet." He then nimbly sketched out a spigot with dollar signs coming out the end and his hand on the handle.

But we had already thought through the money issue. Not only had our school, in fact, made it easier to be married while attending school by way of ridiculously cheap married student housing, but the government had also done its part with the Pell Grant once we would no longer be dependents of our parents. It seemed that everyone but my father thought that there was no reason why we should not tie the knot.

And still, neither of us actually had a job. Destined to become a teen bride so that I could stop feeling guilty for wanting to have sex, I discussed the issue with my roommate, Tracey.

"Y'all should drive a school bus like I do," she told me one morning soon after we announced our engagement. It was morning and she was getting ready for her own route. The "bus barn" was just down the street and apparently had a lot of college kids on the payroll. Good pay and good hours for students.

She whipped out a can of Aqua Net and got to work freeze-framing her locks as she talked. I did the math. It wouldn't take much to live on if we got a small apartment with student housing. At the time, we could get a place for $120 a month on campus. Sure it was 300 square feet and had a view of the cafeteria dumpster, but we could put up curtains. Curtains to shield us from the prying eyes of the cafeteria workers, friends, our pastor and possibly even God Himself so that we could skip from room to room wearing nothing but garlands in our hair.

Lured by the thought of being able to afford a life of marital bliss, one in which coitus came freely and without guilt, Scott and I both signed up for bus driving lessons.

The leader of the bus barn was old, had Marlboro stained creases on his face and appeared to have a lifetime of red meat stored in his gut. He taught us about lug nuts, airbrakes and how to park one of those SOBs backwards into a space with only three feet on either side.

Marcy, the driver I was assigned to was blonde, beautiful, and sang constantly. She was the Cinderella of the bus-driving world. When she stepped outside the bus, all manner of woodland creatures whirled admiringly about her.

"Now put it into third," she would say before trilling into an arpeggio from the seat behind me. I would grab that giant stick shift that came up out of a shaft on the floor and grind it into submission all the while thinking about how I could use that move on Scott once we were married and in our $120 a month student apartment with curtains. Everything was going along smoothly until one day Scott was turning right at an intersection and crunched the car next to him like a can of grape Fanta.

With only one month before we could strap harnesses onto ourselves and swing naked like Julianne Moore in *The Big Lebowski* over the canvas of our love, we were not about to let this little roadblock stop us. Until Mr. Trumbell called me into his office, his Marlboro infused Folgers breath reaching out to me across his desk like tentacles.

"We just ain't got nothing for you this semester," explained Mr. Trumbell. "I got plenty of drivers on a waiting list already. Ones who ain't been in no accidents, neither."

I sat breathing through my mouth, blinking at him.

"But I wasn't in an accident. Scott was."

He shrugged.

"If I can't give him a job, then I can't give you one, neither."

I was stunned. I walked away, tears burning in my eyes. Our teen wedding was planned and waiting for us upon our return home and we weren't going to be able to afford peanut butter, let alone oysters. It was a disaster. What was I supposed to do with all that training? What use were lug nuts and stick shifts without curtains and a front door?

Through great hormonal anguish, we decided that job or no job, we were not going to be able to make it through another hot summer and retain our technical virginity. Thus, our wedding would proceed as planned.

With six floral-printed bridesmaids, six groomsmen, and a church full of onlookers, we said our vows one cloudy July afternoon. We were both 19. A full quarter of the audience was comprised of kids from my high school who were having trouble believing that anyone their age was voluntarily going through with a wedding without a reason that involves a rear-facing car seat. From them I received one dry-mouthed whisper of congratulations after another.

My father could not hide a certain ashen quality to his countenance. His one line in answer to the question, "Who gives Erika to be Scott's bride?" had to be practiced repeatedly in a variety of intonations before he could get the smooth, "Her mother and I do," down, without his voice cracking. Afterwards, he worked the crowd of his friends as amiably and nonchalantly as possible, whilst occasionally casting a glance in my direction to flip his wrist a few times over the proverbial faucet.

By the time we got to the hotel that night, we were exhausted. Well, not too exhausted, but tired enough that by the time it was all over, neither of us was quite sure that it had been worth four and a half years of suspense.

I remember lying there together later that night, cuddled tight. We were so in love. We were also so naïve. We had done everything right, and were now sitting back to claim our blessing. Neither of us could have foreseen the beating our marriage would take over the next several years. How could we have known in that moment that we would later have to claw our way to independence in the face of such an early yoking. That we would be forced to assert our own rights to grow up in the real world after we had left the protection of one that had been manufactured for our safety. In no way were we prepared for it. We had waited, replacing our passion for each other as much as possible with passion for God and jumped into marriage young simply so that we could have sex. When the newness of it wore off with time, it was if we were suddenly faced with a giant question: So, now what? In truth, it almost destroyed us.

●

I Feel Pretty...

As I've said, the church of my youth did a wonderful job relating to us. We learned our modern translation Bible. Listened to our Christian music. Studied our Christian art. Read our Christian books. Took our non-Christian friends to activities like Christian swim nights and Christian camp and Christian prom. We had a Christian version for everything under the sun. We excelled at substitutions. We took every good idea from secular society, made a knock-off version of it for ourselves, and slapped the label "Christian" on it.

One of my favorite Christian substitutions meant to relate to us was in lieu of Halloween. There is not a child in all of Christendom who does not understand at some level that Halloween is the Devil's holiday. Unwittingly, droves of children traipse through the neighborhood streets on Halloween night like they're following the Pied Piper. And we all know who the Pied Piper was patterned after—the Greek demigod, Pan. And Pan, with his hoofed feet and fancy fingered flute stylings is nobody if not the Devil. Children follow along that sweet siren song until they ultimately meet their demise somewhere in their teen years via a drug overdose. And all because parents give into peer pressure and let their kids tango with the Devil for one night every year.

Hence, the church would like to see Halloween banned altogether. Nothing good could possibly come of it. Or... could it? What if there was a way to turn the Devil's holiday upside down? Turn the proverbial upside down pentagram right side up, which would make it...still a pentagram, but try to follow along with me here. The Devil is most effective at drawing children to himself on the strength of cheap costumes and a quick rush of sugar. How does the church rescue all of those innocent children from sliding directly into Satan's candy-coated maw? With cheap costumes and a quick rush of sugar, of course!

I am referring to Fall Fest—Halloween's little brother in highwaters and a pocket protector. And just like your real little brother, this one will tell on you for that snitched sip of hooch from the cabinet, too.

Kids dress up in benign or biblical themed costumes (no witches, ghosts, dead Kenny, etc.) and head on over to the church where they parade through brightly lit hallways, procuring candy as they make stops at various stations (face-painting, crafts, gourd toss, etc.), giggling merrily along the way. There is no chance of being frightened, slashed by that illusive candy-appled razor blade, or bombarded with even so much as a thought about death's red-faced minions. Fall Fest is Halloween in a rubber.

Guide to Churchese

Christian Alternative – This is what is provided by churches to compete with something that is perceived to be ungodly and is siphoning too many of its parishioners off on a regular basis. Examples of this include Christian rock (CCM), Christian radio, Christian fun night, Christian romance novels, Christian bookstores, Christian matchmaking, Christian video games, and Christian yoga.

And although college kids are way too old to be running around the church halls collecting candy, a grown up version of Fall Fest is alive and well on the Christian college campus. As an extension of Youth Group, how could it be any other way? And really, the administration has no choice. Without a Halloween alternative for the kiddos, terrible, destructive things could happen on their watch. For starters, college students might try and trick-or-treat in one of the otherwise quiet nearby neighborhoods, causing grumbling and concern that the school isn't doing its job. Worse, they might have enough time on their hands to attend an unholy haunted house. From there, it's a short jump to doing flaming shots at the House of Gurlz on the edge of town. An alternative must be provided.

Thus is Fall Fest announced each year on the Christian campus. Costumes? Check. Candy? Check. Games and possibly a bonfire? You betcha.

So, when Marcus came to me for help with his costume, I was eager to help. Marcus was one of Scott's best friends and was in most of his science classes with him. Scott and I were married at this point and lived in married student housing—a detail that our friends loved since it was one of the only co-ed hangouts available on campus that was not the library or the student union. While I would be trying to sleep in bed, Marcus and Scott would be sitting up at the desk in our room for hours on end staring at the computer screen. Every so often, one of them would chuckle flatly at something on the screen, letting me know that they were at least partly still in this reality. Raised in Iowa, Marcus had come to Oklahoma as we had with the aid of a scholarship and a promise of a bright and godly education. He was of medium height, thin, and looked like a smarter, more coordinated version of Scooby Doo's pal, Shaggy.

"So, what do you want to be?" I asked him when he came to me for help. We sat in the living room on an overstuffed pastel loveseat, a gift from Scott's mom.

He appeared to think for a moment, stared up at the ceiling, rubbed at some chin scruff.

"I don't know. I thought about maybe going as a Klingon."

"OK..." I looked him over. Marcus is as white as a pilgrim with a rather short forehead. I glanced at his shoulder length hair, though, and thought I saw some promise.

"How much do you want to spend?"

He shrugged, "I don't know." Marcus had the habit of singing this phrase in the back of his throat without the aid of consonants.

"You're going to need dark makeup, a forehead mold... and we'll need to sew you a costume so you look like you just walked off the control deck." This last bit I added somewhat eagerly, as I had just recently acquired a sewing machine.

He sighed and glanced sideways.

"That's a lot of work."

"Well, do you have any better ideas?"

He appeared to think for a moment.

"I could just go as...a girl."

I studied him, a little startled that he had Option 2 so readily available. Finally, I laughed as the comedy of it set in. It was brilliant. He would make a hilarious girl.

As it was the day before Fall Fest would take place, I went straight to my closet to see what I had that could fit him. It would need to be warm since we were going to be outside for the giant bonfire, but I couldn't get around the fact that he needed a skirt if he was going to pull off the look. I shuffled some hangers around in my closet until I came up with a jean skirt and a green blouse. He thanked me and headed into the bathroom.

Thinking he only needed to use the facilities, I was somewhat surprised when he popped out a few minutes later wearing the outfit and a coy grin.

"Do you have shoes?"

I handed him a pair of pumps, into which he crammed his feet like one of Cinderella's wicked stepsisters. They were so small on him that the tops of his feet were bowed into a to-scale model of the St. Louis Gateway Arch. He looked up at me.

"Do you have, like, some eye shadow?"

I wrinkled my face up at him, still amused but with a growing sense of unease.

"Wow—you're really into this dress rehearsal thing," I laughed. "Don't you want to just wait 'til tomorrow night? We're going to eat in an hour."

We had been planning this night at the Olive Garden with friends for about a week. Afterwards, we were going to see the new *Star Trek Next Gen* movie where it occurred to me that we could revisit the Klingon idea. It was a legitimate night out. For dressing up...not across.

He shrugged and sang his consonant-less "I don't know." After a few moments of thought he added, "Can I borrow your razor?"

I headed into the kitchen. Scott wasn't home and I was beginning to feel a little weird about all of this feminine zeal. While he was busy lathering his legs up in the sink, I picked up the phone to call Karen before remembering that she and her roommate, Barbra, had said they were going to take a nap before the evening's outing. I knew better than to disturb their naptime, which—second to chapel—was a sacred time for them. I had called over there once before in the middle of their regular afternoon siesta and had gotten a rather curt response and a click. I supposed this was because they were biology majors and were up all hours of the night studying about dissecting things like frogs and eyeballs.

I replaced the receiver and tried to read a chapter for one of my classes the next day. In a little while, Marcus came prancing out, legs shining like a Gucci handbag.

"What do you think?" he asked, taking a turn in front of the kitchen table.

"Wow," I said honestly.

"Let's practice makeup. Can you teach me what to do?"

I gulped. *What did he want from me?* Wasn't this going too far? I remembered the men with ladies hair in the Satanic backmasking video. What if there were children at Fall Fest?

"You're starting to look a little...convincing."

"I know!" He practically shouted, apparently pleased with the transformation that was underway. "Do you think anybody will know it's me?"

I looked over his bony face and square chin—now minus the scruff—and scratched my head. I returned a sung, "I don't know."

Next thing I knew, we were in the bathroom with me applying foundation, blush, eye makeup, and lipgloss. Spying my curling iron next to the sink, he switched it on.

"Ha ha," I chuckled, applying an Egyptian turn to the corner of his eyes with some brown-black eyeliner. "Now you *really* look hilarious."

He looked at me. Was that hurt in his eyes?

"I think I look pretty convincing," he told me, pouting.

"Um, yeah. Kinda spooky," I returned.

He beamed at me from his position on the closed toilet seat.

When Scott came back later, he found Marcus sitting cross-legged at the edge of the pastel loveseat, flipping through a copy of *Better Homes and Gardens*.

"Are you guys ready to.... Whoa."

Marcus batted his eyes at Scott like Betty Boop. Somewhere between the time we had done his makeup and the time Scott walked in the door, Marcus had managed to create for himself a bosom. It was an ample bosom, and surprisingly... symmetrical. Remembering that I had left a bra to hang on the back of the bathroom door, I stared at him.

A knock at the door interrupted the awkward silence and soon Karen and Barbra had joined Scott in wide-eyed wonder. The two of them looked refreshed from their recent naptime, if not a little stunned. Nobody spoke for quite some time. Finally, Karen broke through the peach-fuzzed haze.

"I call shotgun."

We crammed into the Jeep and drove across town to the Olive Garden. Marcus was in character the whole way, even asking if he should sit on my lap on the ride over since it was so tight in the backseat. When questioned about why he insisted on touching up his makeup in the ladies' room upon arrival, he giggled. It was to check out how credible he looked, he said. If nobody called him on being in the Olive Garden women's bathroom, then he had been a success. Each time somebody would hold a door for him or not stare too long, he would nudge me in the ribs.

"They really think I'm a girl!" He wrinkled up his bushy eyebrows in delight and took a seat in front of a basket of breadsticks.

As happy for him as I was, I was feeling weirder and weirder about it as the night went on. By the time he took the ticket at the movie theater, I couldn't help but notice that he had put a little swish into his step and that he had kicked his voice up a notch. But the most amazing thing to me of all now is this: I did not even have a clue.

It wasn't until a few years ago, as a matter of fact, that I finally got what that was all about. He sent us a rather cryptic email from Amsterdam. It was signed "from Jenny."

Looking back now, I can only guess at the torment he must have had, believing that his outside didn't adequately reflect who he was on the inside. And probably, my current use of pronoun is wrong. I wonder if *she* even understood where she was heading at that point.

Of my six closest friends at the Christian college I ended up attending, three have come out of the closet since graduation. And they're not the only ones. I have since then heard all the dirt to which I was not privy due to my then über-Christian status. Even the boy my mom wanted me to marry for years before I met Scott and who ended up at my university turned out to be gay. And no, I am not a gay magnet, if that's what you're thinking. Just because I adore the Indigo Girls, love to kickbox and drive a Jeep...anyway, back to my immediate group of friends. That's 50% non-hetero. I could be wrong, but the last time I checked, that's way above the national average.

So what gives? Is the Evangelical Christian university a gay factory? I know it sounds ridiculous, but think about it. Is it all that repression? All that: "don't have sex until you're married." Is it the girls staying cloistered in the girls' dorms and the boys' staying cloistered in the boy's dorms? When a person feels homosexual urges, how does a person even know how to behave? Even the rules of "how far to go and when to say no" no longer fully apply. One could argue that it's a pretty slick loophole, don't you think? One might even say that it is a pretty slick *alternative*.

Yeah. I'm just messing with you.

*

When Ted Haggard got busted for regularly sneaking off with a male prostitute and doing meth, and then each other, I was not surprised. Anybody who has spent any amount of time in the Evangelical community should not be surprised either. Not really.

There is a code in the church. Certain rules for behavior. These rules are based on the church's interpretation of scripture and are, in many cases, culturally selective. For example, disobedient children are apparently worthy of stoning in the Gospel of Matthew. The Old Testament says that people who work on the Sabbath are worthy of stoning. This forbidden "work" that is worthy of death includes building a fire, gathering sticks, and even cooking. And yet, what modern Evangelical would not keep his or her family warm on a Sunday? When grandma clicks on the oven to make her famous Sunday pot roast, how many Evangelical families begin searching their rock gardens for the best rocks to thwack her in the head?

Slavery in the Bible is another example of scripture that is viewed as "cultural" today. For example, the Bible says: "If a man beats his male or female slave with a rod and the slave dies as a direct result, he must be punished, but he is not to be punished if the slave gets up after a day or two, since the slave is his property." (Exodus 21:20-21) It is reasonable to assess that the Biblical stance on slaves is that there are some humans—slaves—that are to be considered property. As property, masters can discipline them however they want ... as long as they don't die immediately (within a day or two) as a result. It took three days for that bitch to die? It's all good.

Similarly, the passages that mention homosexuality in the Bible leave some room for interpretation both culturally, as well as linguistically. Several of the verses where the word "homosexual" occurs were not translated from a corresponding word at all. Take for example I Corinthians 6:9:

"...do you not know that the unrighteous will not inherit the kingdom of God? Do not be deceived; neither fornicators, nor idolaters, nor adulterers, nor effeminate, nor homosexuals... I Corinthians 6:9, NASB).

See, it's right there in plain English. It said the homosexuals would not inherit the kingdom of God. Closed case.

But just for the sake of argument, let's look at the same verse in a few other translations:

"Know ye not that the unrighteous shall not inherit the kingdom of God? Be not deceived, neither fornicators, nor idolaters, nor adulterers, nor effeminate, nor abusers of themselves with mankind..." (KJV)

"Or know ye not that the unrighteous shall not inherit the kingdom of God? Be not deceived: neither fornicators, nor idolaters, nor adulterers, nor effeminate, nor abusers of themselves with men..." (ASV)

"Do you not know that unrighteous men will not inherit God's Kingdom? Cherish no delusion here. Neither fornicators, nor idolaters, nor adulterers, nor any who are guilty of unnatural crime..." (Weymouth New Testament)

"Have ye not known that the unrighteous the reign of God shall not inherit? be not led astray; neither whoremongers, nor idolaters, nor adulterers, nor effeminate, nor sodomites..." (Young's Literal Translation)

So, depending on the translation, the same verse says "homosexuals," "abusers of themselves with mankind," "abusers of themselves with men," "any who are guilty of unnatural crime," and "sodomites."

The actual Greek word under debate here is "ἀρσενοκοίτης" (arsenokoites). The word the Greeks normally used for male intercourse was "androkoites." So what was arsenokoites intended to mean? It would seem that linguists don't actually know. It was not used much in writings and, as such, has lost its common meaning. The Greek philosopher Philo in 35 A.D. used it to mean "prostitution." After Philo, the term could be found to refer to all manner of sexual activities, including incest, rape and prostitution. In the 500s it was used in a treatise to indicate sex not intended for procreation. So, by this definition, it would seem I have been practicing "arsenokoites" with my husband for quite some time now.

When Pat Robertson said in a 2012 broadcast that when homosexuals could show him a baby he would back down, he was expressing his belief in the God-given function of sex. For Pat and many like him, sex should only be used for the purpose of baby production. If that cannot be accomplished, then there is no justification. Sex for pleasure is simply not allowed. It is why people in his camp like to point out that homosexuality is contrary to nature—citing that God did not make man for man, but woman for man, and that their love juices should have a purpose.

What they conveniently gloss over, though, is that there are plenty of examples of homosexual behavior in nature. Also ironically glossed over in the "contrary to nature" argument is that the pleasure of sex is pretty much the *cause* of nature. Add to this the fact that a sex differentiation expert is called in for

1 in 1500-2000 births and some researchers say that as high as 9% of the population is born with some noticeable degree of sexual ambiguity in their genitalia, and there is obviously a problem with such a cut and dry interpretation of scripture. Man and woman may have been created for each other as many interpret the story of Adam and Eve to mean, but what happens when a person is born as both a woman and a man—as more than 150,000 Americans currently are? Are we not to believe that their intersex status is real because the Bible did not include someone named Pat or Chris in the Garden of Eden story? And how can we really argue that homosexuality is not just as legitimate?

In the Christian university setting, I watched at point blank range while three of my close friends struggled with their sexual identity. Two of them didn't even know that they were lesbians. They just called their urges "sinning" because this is what the church culture had told them it was. The thought that they could possibly be gay didn't even occur to them because they literally thought that being gay was a choice, even though their wiring indicated otherwise.

Ted Haggard told Oprah, "I am heterosexual with homosexual attachments." He also, apparently, is not gay. When I stated above that I was not surprised at his behavior, I simply meant to imply that church culture has forced him into a mold that his nature seems to deny. *Of course* he had to go underground with his "compulsions." And like the Catholic priests who take vows of abstinence and then end up molesting and raping young boys, repression of one's nature can yield unhealthy behavior.

As a student of linguistics, this debate has meant a lot to me in terms of how I view the Bible and how I view the church culture in which I was raised. Our church was ripe with rules, all of which stood conspicuously by a Bible verse, which seemed to indicate the indisputability of the "rule."

Not every rule, of course. Some rules. Rules that make people uncomfortable. Homosexuality, for example. Not slavery.

To Hell in a Handbasket

On the day the Alfred P. Murrah building exploded in downtown Oklahoma City, I was two minutes late to my Spanish class. The elevator doors had just opened when the boom shook our campus like a small earthquake. Thinking it was maybe a sonic boom from a military flyover, we greeted each other brightly before commencing a lively discussion as to the location of one highly illusive *biblioteca* in relation to its proximity to *el banco*.

Afterwards, we made our way over to chapel, per usual. There it was announced that a building had exploded downtown and that many people had died and even more had been injured. Our chaplin let us know that a few people from the nursing department had been sent to help, but that the rest of us should remain seated because we had a special speaker that day, and boy were we in for a *treat*.

I sat there, frozen, thinking that I had heard him wrong. Had he not just said that people were injured and dying for several blocks around the blast site and that people were scrambling to help? We should be going there to help, too. Maybe we could hand out water bottles. Blankets. Find people who had been hit by glass in the surrounding buildings and who didn't know what to do. Hold an old lady's hand or comfort a confused child.

We had no idea of the scope of the damage at that point. By the time the numbers came in after days of waiting while the heavens opened up and dumped rivers of tears on that city, we were numb with the horror of it. 168 dead. 16 children dead. 3 babies dead who would never be born. In the following days, we would wait through strike after strike of lightning, cringing as the booms rolled through our torn community, wondering if any more survivors could possibly still be found beneath the soggy, blackened wreckage.

But we were not to move. It was time for chapel, and that is where we needed to be. If we left, we were told, we would not get credit that day. Points would be withheld. We all looked around at each other as the university worship team fired up the band and led us in a round of "If God Is for Us, Who Can Be against Us?".

*

I have a bone to pick with Hell.

Truth be told, I love Hell as much as the next person. Specifically, I love to hate Hell. It gives me all manner of scary and indignant feelings. Thoughts of Hell give me focus, as in, "I had better not steal that unattended piece of chocolate because chocolate is not worth an eternity in Hell." Well, maybe some chocolate is, but that's not my point. It also gives me solace to think that people who deserve it will go there. Not me, mind you. *Them*. People like rapists and killers and people who cut in front of me on the highway. Even so, something about the concept of Hell bothers me.

Most Evangelicals think of Hell as a place of eternal torment located "down there" and characterized by separation from God and/or immense heat; the main purpose of

Evangelical Christianity appears to be its avoidance. In the modern translations of the New Testament, there are 12-14 mentions of the word "Hell," depending on which translation you happen to be reading. In the same translations of the Old Testament, there are none.

Adam, Abraham, Jacob, Joseph, Moses, and David had never heard of Hell. They all talked about the afterlife in terms of "Sheol," which means "the grave."

All mentions of Hell by Jesus, with the exception of one,[4] can be translated as "Gehenna." Gehenna is a

Guide to Churchese

Hell — 1. Thought of by most Evangelicals as a place of eternal torment located "down there" and characterized by separation from God and/or immense heat. The main purpose of Evangelical Christianity appears to be avoiding it.

former trash dump on the edge of Jerusalem, located in the Valley of Hinon. It used to have fire incinerators going at all times to dispose of trash, animal waste, and the bodies of criminals. For example, Jesus spoke of it being better to cut off your hand if it does something wrong rather than to have all of you thrown into the fires of "Hell" (Gehenna). Today, Gehenna has been turned into a park. It's lovely. My parents stopped there on vacation once.

Here's the thing. I don't know about an eternal place called "Hell"—I'm not even sure that the modern concept of Hell is biblical—but in the case of the Oklahoma City bombing, Hell was right down the highway with people begging for volunteers and we were rerouted from helping a single person so that we could have a treat.

A Scooby snack for the soul.

---

4   * The one exception is "Hades." You know...the Greek afterlife where Persephone spends half the year while it winters in the northern temperate zone?

MAIDS EN MASSE

Upon leaving the comfortable, too-crowded nest of a Christian university in Oklahoma, Scott and I took the next logical step available to us: we packed our bags, got on a plane, and moved to a small backpacker island in the South China Sea.

We were looking for something different than anything we had experienced before. Something more gritty. In a way, we felt that we had missed something going to the Christian university. As if the Christian university was a substitute for a real one. I'm not saying that the academics were subpar. On the contrary, I felt well-equipped with the bookcase I had stocked with Faulkner, Wordsworth and Tennyson. I could concrete over an abstraction. Deconstruct a dialectic. It was more that it felt as if we had been protected from something. It was as if we were still in, well, Youth Group.

And so we chose the most unusual situation that we could conceive of: graduate school in Hong Kong. While Scott studied Molecular Bioinformatics during the week, I worked on my Masters Degree in the highly useful field of Postcolonial Literature and Linguistics.

While I loved the experience of living in Asia, it was difficult being so far away from what I was used to. Everything in my life was different: the people, the transportation, the food…and especially Sundays.

When we first arrived, I looked for a church I could attend. Having come from the heart of Evangelicalism, I may have been frustrated with the way I witnessed my church handling certain things, but I was still keenly aware of what I ought to be doing—going there on Sundays, regardless. I figured I would run into some sort of problem finding the right place for me: not enough young people, too charismatic, too liturgical, too stuffy, too far away. The last reason I ever thought I would have trouble locating a church was that I would have to navigate my way through crowds of maids.

Guide to Churchese

Evangelicalism – 1. The art of being an Evangelical. 2. A political platform calling all Americans to remember their Christian heritage—regardless of their actual heritage—thus inspiring the return of prayer in schools to the one, true God and the death of Darwin once and for all.

They were everywhere. Mostly hailing from the Philippines, the legions of domestic workers sat on red, white, and blue tarps and were in every corner of every outdoor public place talking, laughing, eating, and sometimes singing. It was their one day off from serving Hong Kong's wealthy and they spent it en masse. They also spent it *in mass*. Many of them had attended church earlier and wore appropriate Sunday attire.

A person could get from place to place, but it wasn't easy. Pushing through a mob anywhere is not a pleasant experience, so when you add to that the factors of a 40-minute breakfast-raising ferry ride, air that makes you feel as if you are being smothered by a towel soaked in diesel, multiple public transportation stops involving subway, minibus, taxi, as well as an inability to speak the language, one frequently is compelled to stay home. Church takes a backseat somehow.

I began to alter my plan. Rather than go to an actual service, I began to take the time to sit and be still. I would maybe take a chair up onto the roof, from where I could see the water's edge around the island. Sometimes I would walk down to the beach, nodding at the locals and the small children playing. It was life as usual for them, but I began to see things that I might not otherwise have noticed. The cadence of mahjong tiles through an open window. The electric glow of backlit indigo through sunlit petals spilling over the concrete walls. The knocking of cane in the breeze. The call and answer of tropical birds. The smell of the sea mixed with plants so green they vibrated in the sunlight. The truth of it.

At the beginning, I had been praying hard that I would find a church situation that would work for me. But despite numerous attempts amongst the maids, I never found it. What I found instead—through my unanswered prayer—was beautiful.

Life on an island in the South China Sea. During the rush of the week it so often felt like a distraction—like it was part of the distance through which I had to travel to get where I wanted to be. But on those Sunday mornings with nothing else to do, I relaxed. I recognized the grace of living on an island outside of the madness of life in a pulsing metropolis. I hadn't gone looking for it or asking for it. As a matter of fact, I had been asking for quite the opposite. It was there all the same. I didn't know what it was teaching me about God or my search for God, but I knew that I needed to pay attention.

God is a DJ

The idea of God is one that I was fed since my conception and the thought of there not being one is automatically rejected at my core. There is a verse in the New Testament that says that everyone knows that there is a God,[5] so I assumed throughout my youth that everyone else felt at their cores that God exists, too. When my friend Chloe told me that she could not even conceive of God, I naturally assumed that she was lying. Maybe not deliberately, but to herself, perhaps. Even agnostic Mary could not say for sure. Everyone knew at some level that God was real. Didn't they?

During the week, I ferried over to the city where I worked on my graduate studies. On weekends, I hung out with Scott and our friends, people from all walks of life from all over the world. For the first time in my life, I had close friends who were heathens: Buddhists, atheists, wine drinkers, hash smokers, and drug dealers. We were a long ways away from Youth Group.

Chloe was young, blonde, British. We became friends through a wing chun kung fu class we were taking. Already

---

5   * Romans 1:19-20 "Since what may be known about God is plain to them, because God has made it plain to them. For since the creation of the world God's invisible qualities—his eternal power and divine nature—have been clearly seen, being understood from what has been made, so that people are without excuse."

I was on my guard due to the nature of kung fu. Kung fu deals with the taking and giving of energy, an ideology that runs uncomfortably against the grain of my Evangelical hairs. Evangelicals generally get antsy around talk like that, often citing New Age philosophy and an assumption that any sort of perceived "energy" emanating from or through the human body must be demonic at its roots. As it would turn out, the church's warnings against such groups of people who practice such things would not be wholly unwarranted. For the first time in my life, I would meet somebody who would profoundly challenge my understanding of God.

Chloe and I would frequently spend the days wandering the paths together. We talked about everything. On the day she tossed this bomb at me, we had been for a swim in the ocean and were returning to grab a bite to eat.

She was unapologetically beautiful with ocean damp hair and breasts that pressed two dark spots into her pink camisole. Light freckles on her nose matched her sand-crusted toes and she walked the leaf-shadowed path as if she bore the weight of a hidden royal past.

Around us on all sides were the spinning dementia of cicadas and the love affairs of bullfrogs. Nature saturated the damp air. We passed from the trees into the cane forests and out past a chicken yard where the hens bickered openly and the cock was king.

We spoke of love and culture and sex and God. She had been raised in the same British boarding school as Cat Stevens. Oh yes, she remembered the old schoolyard. Our conversation, like our path, meandered heavily.

Love is a battlefield.
Culture is a club.
Sex is natural.
God is a DJ.

We passed under a cicada mist and our faces moistened with their sticky insanity. She told me that she loved me, without shame. She had love to spare. She was beautiful— is beautiful still—in my memory. I took her arm and called her sister. She made me feel beautiful by association. The kind of beauty that doesn't care if every hair is in place or whether blemishes show. That kind of beauty is rare. From the soul. Within.

Guide to Churchese

Heathen – If you are not an Evangelical Christian, then... well...this would be you.

She didn't believe in God, she said. She told me that she used to ask the nuns at her school to explain things and got rapped on the knuckles by a wooden ruler on more than one occasion. She said she could not even conceive of God. At night, she lay awake trying to imagine one. She wanted to pray to God, to find God, but had come up empty.

I didn't know what to say. How to respond. I honestly thought that everybody knew that there was a God. Sure, I had heard of atheists, but I figured they did not believe because they did not want to. Chloe wanted to, and still she could not.

After several months of me chipping away at the subject, her expression began to change. She wasn't looking at me filled with empathy for my lack of understanding anymore, she was genuinely distraught.

"I don't know why I can't conceive of God," she would tell me, eyebrows knitted with worry. "I want to, I really do. What's wrong with me?"

I backed off. I hadn't meant to alarm her. It's just that I had never met someone like her before. I had heard people say that they didn't care about the idea of God. I had heard people say that God is a social construct and that there is no proof. I had even heard people say, "If God exists, then He is unjust and I don't want any part of Him." But what she was saying was different. What she was saying rocked my very foundation.

One night, Chloe and I stood together on the shore of the South China Sea. Before us, the ocean hushed on the downbeat while we practiced the forms of our art. Slowly, we speared and parried our energy into the breeze and then back upon ourselves.

Tan sau. Fuk sau. Bong sau.

Others in our class spread out around and behind us. Before us was the inky green of the ocean at night, rhythmic and regular in its white-tipped entropy.

Tan sau. Fuk sau. Bong sau.

Take energy. Give energy. Round and back again.

My eyes focused beyond the black over the water, not understanding what I was seeing at first. It was the crest of a wave. A piece of trash. An angel on the breeze. It floated toward me, drifting with design.

Upon realizing that this other-worldly thing was alive, I moved toward it, leaving the rest of my class behind me on the higher sand. I was compelled toward it. Its glowing wings flowed and rippled as if slack on their frames. Tassles hung from them, spread wider than the diameter of my hand from thumb to pinky. It was beautiful. *My God*, it was beautiful. It must have been a large moth, but it hardly seemed as if it could be from this earth. Who would believe me? Was it actually a moth? It was so big. I wanted to touch it. I wanted to be blessed by it and learn from it. I reached for it. Inches from my hand, I could see it. Our souls connected and my blood paused in its channels. I felt it then—its energy, its purity. Its wings as beautiful as infant's breath. Its large, dark eyes as black and terrifying as the night sky. It pierced me to my core, the truth of it.

And yet, just as it was about to land on my finger, I withdrew my hand out of fear. I cursed myself for my own weakness. For the opportunity lost. I returned slowly toward my class, and walked back up the beach.

Many years later I would visit my friend in her London home. Much had happened in the time since we had last seen each other. She would take me around. We would get pasties and beer; would go to a few bookstores. She would take me to the tower where we would stare at the flightless ravens and dare them to say to us the only word they presumably knew. At night, we would lie under her pink satin bed cover and listen to an Indian guru she had studied under while he chanted in a language I could not begin to understand. She would turn to me to tell me she believed in God now. Maybe not completely, but she was trying.

For the first time in my life, I understood just what she meant.

THE CHURCH

AND SO BEGAN A PERIOD OF UNRAVELING. THAT IT TOOK until my mid-20s when I *actually* rebelled is a small miracle, considering. But there was a lot I had to learn. Or unlearn, rather. And then learn again. I became an experience-collector. I drank wine. I went dancing. I drank wine and went dancing. I dabbled in yoga. I crossed over into kung fu. I became a fighter. I beat up an old lady once. I learned to say the word *fuck*. I learned to jump out of an airplane. I learned to say the word *fuck* and jump out of an airplane, *at the same time*. I messed up my marriage and then returned to it. I had kids. I continued to mess up my marriage. I am very good at messing up my marriage. I went to raves. I dressed up in a dog collar and hacked up a refrigerator with an axe in front of a crowd at midnight in a junkyard once. I drank beer before wine and felt...just fine. Some of it was good for me; some of it wasn't, but my operating theory was that I wouldn't know unless I had tried. I had never been allowed to mess up before. I was tired of having people tell me what was OK and what would land me in a charred cell. I needed to mess up. I needed the freedom to mess up. I needed the freedom—and the courage—to stare that giant white moth in the black, beady eyes.

Even so, there was a moment in my adult years when I knew I was in trouble. I had crossed the line with experimentation and had exposed myself for what I truly was: once an Evangelical, always an Evangelical. No matter what I did, there was no escaping my past. Not totally, anyway.

I was at The Church in downtown Denver. For anyone not familiar, The Church is a nightclub that holds raves within its former sanctuary. Inside The Church, overhead lighting throws sparkles over the otherwise darkened swarms of bodies twisting and thumping while the altar at the head of the former sanctuary blazes red with candles. Past the sanctuary, into a former common room, a live band plays next to a jam-packed bar. Below that, down in the undercroft, you'll find even darker music next to an even darker smoking room.

Guide to Churchese

Backsliding – 1. The slippery slope backwards from being right with God through a pattern of sinful behavior. For the Calvinist, it may provide evidence that you were never saved at all. Applies to Presbyterians, some Baptists, etc. 2. A vital component to the shampoo method of salvation: Rinse and Repeat. Applies to Methodists, Nazarenes, Church of Christ, other Baptists.

Yeah, so that's where I was.

At the time, I was involved with a group of friends from a martial arts dojo in which I was training. We did everything together, and by every*thing* I mostly mean every *night*. There was a core component to the group, with the majority of us girls in our 20s. We were hot and dangerous, or so we thought. I mean, it wasn't like we thought we were The Charlie's Angels or anything (yes we did), but we managed to have a good time. Scott was also with us that night, although we did not exactly keep close tabs on each other in those days. He might have wandered up the street and I would have been none the wiser.

The scene down in the undercroft was what you might expect. From the moment you entered the room, you were hit in the face by a Rob Zombie shovel, grabbed by the shoulders and thrown into a gyrating mosh pit on the dance floor. It was dark, and it was glorious.

Of course, I didn't get it.

Not really, anyway. As an official experience-collector who also happens to be making up for lost time, I am usually one step removed from whatever scene I happen to throw myself into. I stood swaying off the floor for several minutes with friends while we shouted comments at each other only to bend double over our drinks, laughing. When I spotted him, I thought I had died and gone to Heaven. Or, more accurately, Hell.

We all agreed he was cute. Unfortunately, he was dressed in a black cape, had his jet black hair slicked straight back, and took himself entirely too seriously. It was clear, he fancied himself an individual. A loner. He was a on a search for a lack of meaning in life through self-discovery and an aggressive depletion of Vitamin D, and he was skipping-not-dancing, weaving-not-darting throughout the crowd like a dark Sith Lord at a Maypole dance. And I just couldn't help it.

Giggling wildly, I ran out onto the floor after him. As I got closer, I could see he had a black tear painted on his white powdered cheek. He needed cheering up. I would cheer him up. I worked my way up right behind him and grabbed him at the waist. He jumped and twirled away from me in an attempt at escape, but I was undaunted. He got stuck at a block in the crowd and I began kicking. Right then left. Right then left. Some girl wearing shredded stockings and a scrap of Mylar stuck to her breasts grabbed on to my waist from behind and started copying my moves. The bottleneck loosened and we went skipping after him, kicking as we went. More people joined on. Ten. Twenty. We followed him, this poor distraught soul. If he twirled in an evasive maneuver, we twirled with him. If he shot us a shriveling glare over his shoulder, we would *vogue* like the Material Girl in response. We added kicks. Hip thrusts. Whatever it took. We would turn this fallen angel into a risen demon if it took us all night.

Looking back now, I realize my mistake. I was trying to relate with him, although I'm sure he thought we were only mocking him. But mocking was the last thing on my mind. I had seen him looking all sad and death-obsessed and like he was ready to start threatening people with lines from his own bad poetry and all I really wanted to do was to cheer him up. Show him a little fun. Show him that life wasn't so hard if you worked together as a group. We would hold him up as a community by first relating to him and then expose him to some good old-fashioned goofy fun. And who can resist goofy fun?

SPIRITUAL VACUUM

THE ADULT VERSION OF ME IS NOT AN EXCEPTIONALLY GOOD person. I get it.

When it comes to my expectations of the Great Beyond, I try not to get too excited. If I make it to Heaven, I'll be doing well to get a studio flat with a dumpster-side view of the Golden Chariot Highway. And I'll be grateful.

If, however, the Ever After is karma-based, death will not bring me peace, for I have work to do. No, not peace; only a new uniform in the grand roller derby we call life.

A few more turns to take in the mortal skin.

A few more rounds of puberty.

A few more high school graduations and potential conflict with my future mothers and fathers.

*

It's been a long road from there to here. Don't get me wrong, I feel I am a long ways off from my destination. I'm the last person to claim that I've arrived. All that I know for sure is that I'm not *there* anymore.

So, what is it about my years with the Evangelical church? Why the uneasy feeling when I look back?

Comedian Sarah Silverman recently made a public challenge to the pope: sell the Vatican and use the money to solve world hunger. Silverman points out that since he preaches to live humbly he should sell his "house that is a city," still build a beautiful condominium—complete with waterslide—for him and all his friends, and be a world hero. It's a brilliant suggestion. And it will never happen.

While her challenge was made to the pope, her suggestion is one that ought to strike a chord with people who claim to be followers of Christ the world over. All of my life I have heard people make accusations of "hypocrisy" toward the church. But as a good Evangelical girl, I never saw it beyond a few isolated events. I was good. I did everything more or less by the book. I gave my heart to Jesus and let him cleanse my soul.

The church taught us well what to do in order to save our souls. In the Arminian tradition from whence I hail, I applied that method frequently: Born again. Rinse. Repeat. I watched my every step constantly to make sure that I was still following the narrow path that would lead me to salvation. I was good at it. I moved with grace. I attempted to bring others with me. I used margarine instead of butter. I rarely stepped out of line.

My soul was nurtured and cared for. I took it to church two or three times a week where I meditated on spiritual things and sang beautiful songs that helped me to reach an emotional state of ecstasy. At the Christian school, I took my soul to classes where I learned to spout verses on demand, along with what I believed to be airtight theological arguments. I saw the world through metaphors and clung to the safety of the answers they provided. In chapel, I took my soul to delicious banquets of rhetoric and thought. At home, I spent time daily on my knees and with my Bible, contemplating what God was trying to say to me and how He was blessing me in ways that I did not even recognize. I bathed my soul. I washed my soul. I scrubbed behind my soul's ears and under my soul's nails.

I pampered the hell out of my soul.

The thing is, I have this itching feeling that there is more. Actually, not more, but less. Maybe more and less. I'm not really sure.

If the Youth Group primarily functioned as a substitute for sex as I have claimed, then what happens once the deed is done and the mystery is laid open? What happens when the youth who are steeped in the safety of Christian programs finally get out into the real world and discover...that it's the real world? That it's messy and artistic and filled with joy and suffering and unanswerable mysteries.

So many of us have left the church. Is it good? Bad? It's not my place to make that judgment. But here's the thing: no matter how much marketing goes into it, at the end of the day, butter will always be victorious over margarine, bacon will beat out Sizzlean, and an honest, individualized search for truth will triumph over a religious system based on the glut of one's soul on substitutions.

While some church communities have done a much better job offering something real than others, some of us feel that we have emerged from a plastic bubble. The experiences we were given too manufactured; the answers we were given too clichéd.

Feed the hungry. Clothe the poor. Take care of those who need it. Relieve the burdens of others. This is true nourishment. This is what is *real*. The problem for me is quite simply that the larger Evangelical culture has gotten away from this somehow and it has become impossible for me to overlook the disconnect. The core message of Jesus—that there is no law above loving God and your neighbor as yourself—has been twisted so thoroughly that it looks a whole lot more like: glut your soul with pep talks, if you have any cravings for life on earth use these approved substitutes, prioritize the saving of souls over destitute bodies, decorate your buildings, and then go there and hide. Oh, and if anyone calls you on it, they are possessed.

I have nothing against the individual people in the Evangelical church. I love my Evangelical family and friends. I love the loving community that they embody. I derive inspiration from watching them thrive in their own journeys within the church. And, I suspect many of them have unlocked some of the secrets for which I am still looking. Within the church are people who actually get the message they support and are generous to their core toward the needs of others. What I am addressing is a culture, which left unchecked, threatened to steal my very soul.

For myself, I have some work to do. Some things I need to learn outside the cultural formula. To figure that out for myself I need fresh air, time for reflection, a warm sun and a fresh mountain breeze on my face. I need the freedom to doubt and the sting of pain to help me understand my boundaries. I need to accept who I am now and the journey I have taken to get here. I need the wisdom to know that I have not yet arrived. I need to include my fellow travelers into what I call "church," regardless of whether we agree on the roadmap. I need to make my *religion* be relief of the pain and suffering of others and my *faith* be a hope that propels me toward an honest quest for that entity we call 'God'. I need to learn to forgive myself and drop any spiritual baggage I may have so that I can become the person I was meant to be.

When faced with embarrassing or uncomfortable moments of our past, a lot of us either go storming off on a mission to derail the system that led us to act that way, or we simply switch off interest altogether. And still, others of us find a way to seek truth in a quieter manner. Perhaps not without faith, exactly, but maybe without the certainty of the definitions we once possessed. But whatever the method, the past is usually not far behind, with all of the old guilt and superstitions just waiting to reappear at the most inappropriate times.

I still believe in God. At least, most days I do. Not that I could tell you with any measure of certainty who or what this entity is to whom I refer as "God." It's not so much a problem of belief in God's existence, it's more a problem of definition. Male? Female? Neither? Both? Source of Love? Smiter of foreign villages? Understanding of my frailties? Intolerantly jealous? Fascinated Switchboard Operator? Laissez-faire? Cognizant Being? Indifferent Life Force? Possessor of the world's longest beard? All of the above? I just don't know.

Even so, I want to.

This moves me forward .

*

I have a painful memory of a conversation with my father before he died. I had just given birth to my oldest daughter and my mom and dad were visiting. Dad was expressing concern over my current church attendance over breakfast. I'd say it was over my "lack of church attendance," but that's not entirely true. I had, as a matter of fact, found a church. The only problem was that he did not exactly approve of my choice of church. But after years of separating in my own mind the pieces of madness from my youth from what I perceive to be the actual message of God's love, it was just what I needed at that time in my life. It made me feel real. I could seek God genuinely there.

So, over French toast, I listened as he told me how great a certain church was in our area and how wonderful it would be if I went there. I pointed out that I had found a place where I was comfortable, but it was clear that he had his doubts about my church, which was far too liberal for either of my parents' liking.

I cleared the table biting back tears of frustration and tried to move on with my day. He loved me, after all. He was only trying to protect my soul. How could he understand the journey that had brought me to this place?

When he tracked me down in the laundry room a couple of hours later to ask me if I'd given any thought toward the other church after living in what he called "a spiritual vacuum" for so long, something inside of me clicked.

The fact that he had used the metaphor of a vacuum to describe my spiritual thoughts and environment was the most troubling to me in that moment. A vacuum. Sealed emptiness. Devoid of space. I had given myself space, this much is true, but I felt there was nothing either closed or empty about it. I had allowed my mind to see things it had never noticed before. I had allowed in new ideas and possibilities. I had given it sunshine and water. And in the end, I had discovered that God—whoever God may be—is so much bigger than anything I could contain by a simple definition, idea, or rule set. It seemed to me that I was breaking the seal and destroying the vacuum that my mind previously was.

What I could not explain to him no matter how hard I tried was that in order to move forward, I needed to back off from my Evangelical past. The problem I was experiencing lay within me, not so much a singled-out institution that I happened to have been a part of. As much as was possible, I needed to do a hard reset. There was too much confusion and I had too many unanswered questions. And there were things that I had become uncomfortable with. Maybe I would see things his way again some day and maybe I would not—but I had to take a true journey and find out for myself. It was the biggest step of faith I would ever make.

I am not proud of what happened next. I laid into him. Hard. In tears, I tried to explain, but I am sorry to say that it came out coated in a bitter shell of anger. I told him that I had made mistakes in my life, but that they were mine to make. I had to make them—*I had to be allowed to make them*—in order to learn from them. I told him that *he* was living in a vacuum. It was my life. I only wished he could stop being so judgmental toward me and respect that.

It was one of the last lucid conversations I had with him before the brain tumor took over his thoughts and personality. Over the next few months, I watched him decline until that final night when I sat alone with him by his bed and watched him go. I loved him so deeply. He had lived what he believed and only wanted what he thought was best for me. As I watched my father die, taking his final gasps as he fought to live in the face of the inevitable, my thoughts were of that conversation in the laundry room. Yes, I wished I could have had his understanding. Yes, I wished I could have had his approval. But more than anything, I wished I could have had his forgiveness—not for thinking differently about God and the church than he did, but forgiveness for being as judgmental of him as I was claiming he was being of me. Whether either of us recognized it at the time, we were still on this path together. *All of us, on this path together.* He taught me that.

ACKNOWLEDGMENTS

One humbling lesson I have learned about publishing: it does not happen alone.

To my Scott: you have gone through years of your life and gallons of espresso bouncing around ideas and re-reading different versions of this book. Thanks for sticking with me, even when things got rough. Here's to nearly two-thirds of our lives together and counting. I promise to love you even after we're too stooped to reach that chandelier.

Special and heartfelt thanks to you, Mom, for your gentle spirit in the face of my restless one. Thank you for your support throughout this process. To my father who now has answers: I love you and I can't wait to pick back up the debate. To my mom and dad-in law, who love me even when I swim against the current: I love you back and thank you for your strength. To my two sisters, I love you no matter what.

To Bryan Tomasovich, my editor who made this happen: you've not only helped me fulfill what has seemed at times an illusive dream, but you have shaped it into the best possible kind: vivid, succinct, and 99% jazz-free.

Brad Listi: you gave me my first entrance into the writers' world through your literary love child, The Nervous Breakdown. This book is at least partly your fault.

Lance Reynald: none of this would have happened without you pointing me in the right direction in the first place.

Nick Belardes: you've been an invaluable mentor to me. I am grateful that our paths crossed.

J.M. Blaine: you give me hope for all of us sinners and questioners. You once told me:

> *There was this blue collar guy*
> *about two thousand years ago*
> *who questioned doctrine*
> *& church culture*
> *& was a friend to outlaws and cheats and addicts and whores*
> *but gave the religious people hell.*

Karyn Dundorf: your thoughtful feedback has been invaluable. Thank you for not liking this book just because you're my friend (or at least for saying that wasn't the reason).

I am grateful for criticism and encouragement that went above and beyond from: Nina Andaloro, Kevin and Aimee Archer, Juliette Leon Bartsch, Beanie Brady, Sarah Branham, Ben Brink, Carissa Carter, Sal and Karen Devincenzo, Megan DiLullo, Slade Ham, Emma Hardy, Stan James, Bridget and Matt Johnson, Alison Marlan, Ben Monlezun, Ursula Monlezun, Amy Moreland, Kirstin and

Todd Orwig, Jason Servetar, Connie Shaw, Jon Skaggs, Ryan Skaggs, Rachel Vater, Kathryn Whitt, and Christine Williams.

To the many, many authors and friends at The Nervous Breakdown who have created a giant frosted writers' community of dysfunctional perfection: in a very real way, we did this together. Thanks to the following misfits for letting me try out pieces of this book and for taking time out of your days to banter, laugh, and inspire. Gina Frangello, Greg Olear, Jessica Anya Blau, Jonathan Evison, J.M. Blaine, Rich Ferguson, Lenore Zion, Megan DiLullo, Uche Ogbuji, Slade Ham, Sean Beaudoin, Simon Smithson, Joe Daly, Thomas Philips, Gloria Harrison, Don Mitchell, Ben Loory, David S. Wills, Susan Henderson, Irene Zion, Zara Potts, Tom Hansen, Quenby Moone, Reno J. Romero, Stefan Kiesbye, Michelle J. Fievre, Andrew Nonadetti, Robin Antalek, Cynthia Hawkins, D.R. Haney, Jeffrey Pillow, Kimberly M. Wetherell, Tawni Freeland, Tyler Stoddard Smith, Matt Baldwin, Becky Palapala, Bradley Parker, James D. Irwin, Marni Grossman, Brin-Jonathan Butler, Chiwan Choi, Oksana Marafioti, Nathaniel Missildine, Judy Prince, Darci Ratliff, Art Edwards, Lauren Becker, Justin Benton, Elizabeth Collins, Stacy Bierlein, Lisa Rae Cunningham, Kip Tobin, Angela Tung, Aaron Dietz, Ronlyn Domingue, Kristen Elde, Jim Simpson, Steve Sparshott, Eric Spitznagel, Will Entrekin, Jennifer Duffield White, Ducky Wilson, David Wozmak, Josie Renwah, Brandon "PhatB" Parris, Tony DuShane...and so many more.

Special thanks to Jorge Bannister, who has for years now maintained his position as quite possibly my one and only unobligated fan. Jesus Pumpkin sends blessings.

To the ladies of my book clubs, past and present: thanks for turning a blind eye when I showed up without having read the book due to being in the middle of writing.

To my Cowgirls: I couldn't ask for a finer roundup of gals. Don't squat with yer spurs on and never ever sell yer saddles.

To Jim C. and Brad D.: you will always rock in my book.

green press

INITIATIVE

Emergency Press participates in the Green Press Initiative. The mission of the Green Press Initiative is to work with book and newspaper industry stakeholders to conserve natural resources, preserve endangered forests, reducd greenhouse gas emissions, and minimize impacts on indigenous communities.

The production of *Devangelical* was supported by the Antioch Media and Publishing Center in Seattle.

Emergency Press thanks Leah Rae Hunter and Frank Tomasovich for their generous support.

RECENT BOOKS FROM EMERGENCY PRESS

Gentry, by Scott Zieher

Green Girl, by Kate Zambreno

Drive Me Out of My Mind, by Chad Faries

Strata, by Ewa Chrusciel

Various Men Who Knew Us as Girls, by Cris Mazza

Super, by Aaron Dietz

Slut Lullabies, by Gina Frangello

American Junkie, by Tom Hansen

EMERGENCY PRESS

emergencypress.com
info@emergencypress.org

ERIKA RAE is editor-in-chief at *Scree Magazine* and nonfiction editor at The Nervous Breakdown, the popular literary site. Erika earned her M.A. in Literature and Linguistics at the University of Hong Kong. A resolute member of the Evangelical church in the American Bible belt since childhood, she started on the path to the Devangelical as a young adult. She lives in Boulder, Colorado with her husband and three children.

CPSIA information can be obtained at www.ICGtesting.com
Printed in the USA
BVOW031649281012

304101BV00002B/13/P